AF681281

ACCELERATE

HOW TO REACH FINANCIAL FREEDOM FASTER SO YOU CAN LIVE THE LIFE YOU WANT

ACCELERATE

HOW TO REACH FINANCIAL FREEDOM FASTER SO YOU CAN LIVE THE LIFE YOU WANT

SCOTT JARRED

ethos collective

ACCELERATE © 2024 by Scott Jarred. All rights reserved.

Printed in the United States of America

Published by Ethos Collective™
PO Box 43, Powell, OH 43065
www.ethoscollective.vip

This book contains material protected under international and federal copyright laws and treaties. Any unauthorized reprint or use of this material is prohibited. No part of this book may be reproduced or transmitted in any form or by any means, electronic or mechanical, including photocopying, recording, or by any information storage and retrieval system, without express written permission from the author.

LCCN: 2023915828
Paperback ISBN: 978-1-63680-205-3
Hardcover ISBN: 978-1-63680-206-0
e-book ISBN: 978-1-63680-207-7

Available in paperback, hardcover, e-book, and audiobook.

Any Internet addresses (websites, blogs, etc.) and telephone numbers printed in this book are offered as a resource. They are not intended in any way to be or imply an endorsement by Ethos Collective™, nor does Ethos Collective™ vouch for the content of these sites and numbers for the life of this book.

Some names and identifying details may have been changed to protect the privacy of individuals.

Table of Contents

Follow this QR Code to access exclusive bonus content.

A Note to the Reader

From Fear to Freedom

What is freedom?

Well, it means something different for everyone. But I can tell you what it means to me—because I spent a long time not being free, living in scarcity, afraid to embark on the journey to get to the life I truly wanted to live.

I was born in Danville, Illinois, and raised in Indianapolis. My parents split when I was in kindergarten, and my family shrank from a poor family of five to an even poorer family of four. When my father left the picture, he was unable to provide my mother with any financial support, and we were forced to move from our apartment to government subsidized Section 8 housing and had to rely on food stamps for food.

My mom worked multiple jobs waiting tables, but money was still a struggle. We were fighting just to survive. Food was so scarce my mom would protect us by locking our food up so we wouldn't accidentally run out before the monthly stipend came in. She would leave me at home alone while she worked, watching over my brother and sister, both in diapers, even though I was only seven and eight years old. I had strict instructions never to leave the house for fear of the drugs, gangs, and abuse that were right outside the door. We had no luxuries, not even cable TV, so the time passed slowly.

I grew up hiding, poor, and afraid—but the hardships my family and I experienced did not crush me. Instead, they sparked in me two burning desires: a desire for money, and a desire for freedom. Lack of money and lack of freedom became my drivers, my big *Why*s, motivating me to figure out how to make opportunities for myself in any way I could.

When my family moved out of subsidized housing and into the suburbs, I caught my first glimpse of another kind of life: a life of abundance. And I knew that was the life I wanted to live. Getting my own paper route and cleaning carpets as a teenager were my first steps toward something better. Football was my ticket into college, and shortly after, my environment changed again when I enrolled at Ball State University and joined a fraternity. The first in my family to graduate from college, I maximized every credit hour I could get, from economics to entrepreneurship to architecture to urban planning. I got my master's in technology and a great first job as a tech consultant for AT&T.

For the first time, I had money—but I still didn't feel free. Corporate America stifled a fire somewhere in me. I wasn't satisfied, I wasn't yet living the life I wanted, because I wasn't helping people. I realized I wanted to make a bigger impact. I didn't want to help large companies become better—I wanted to help people become better. I wanted to help people with their financial stability, independence, and financial future—the same things I wanted for myself. I believed if I could help people take control of their finances and make money, I could make a difference in people's lives. So, at 26 years old, I took a leap of faith and launched JarredBunch Consulting.

Fast forward to 2016. I'm 39, financially secure through my investments, and after almost two decades of accumulating specialized knowledge as a wealth advisor I've reached the pinnacle of my industry: Top 10 in our company multiple years in a row, one of the most successful wealth advisors in the country, with countless lessons about managing money I'd learned personally from the truly wealthy. And I am still not free. In fact, I am very much bound, by golden handcuffs, to a life that isn't truly the life I want to live.

As an affiliate representative of a broker-dealer, I was contractually obligated to be a salesperson for their products. The problem was, I felt many of their products were garbage and provided more benefit to the institution than to the client. I couldn't in good conscience recommend them to my clients. Despite the "wealth" of knowledge I'd accumulated, I couldn't advise people on how I truly believed they should manage their money.

I wanted to start my own wealth management firm—but if I left, I would lose a multi-million-dollar pension set to pay me two million dollars a year, as well as $500,000 in a wealth accumulation plan and $500,000 in annual renewals. That is a heck of a lot of money to walk away from.

I could feel the fear taking hold of me—the same fear that kept us locked in the house with a padlock on the fridge when I was a kid. At this point, I understood this was a mindset of scarcity—but I still had that voice from my childhood in my head saying, "You can't possibly let go of that much money! Don't set out on some foolhardy journey to who knows where! Stay where you are!"

Unsure what to do, I explained my predicament to my associate, Lloyd Easters.

"Look, Scott," Lloyd said, when I'd laid out the whole situation. "Say you're holding a glass of water, and there's a pitcher sitting on the table. If you want to pick up that pitcher of opportunity, which is full of so much more water, you have to set down the glass of scarcity first. You have to laugh and let it all go."

I knew he was right. I knew the only way I could be truly free was to quit. I had to write my own story, embark on my own journey. Only then could I truly live the life I wanted.

So I did.

In June 2016, I founded Invst along with my integrator, Lloyd. Now, we were forever free to sit on the same side of the table as our clients as true fiduciaries, offering and implementing financial strategies that we know will radically help our clients live the life they want. We could change the entire game.

I believed with all my being in this mission, and it has paid off. Within a few months, we were managing $100 million in assets. In 2023, Invst had billions of assets, information, and permanent life insurance under management, a $300 million real estate portfolio that pays monthly cash flows to investors, and we help many business owners scale, maximize value, and exit while leaving a legacy for their family.

I am deeply grateful to be able to help so many people achieve what I thirsted for myself for so long: freedom. Now, I want to share those principles and strategies with you, so you too can begin your journey toward financial freedom and accelerate to the life you want for yourself, your family, and your future.

Introduction

The Journey

Imagine, stretching out before you, an open road: a journey into the future. You don't know what exactly lies along this road, where it may curve, what obstacles or roadside attractions might be along the way. But you know one thing for sure: at the end of that road, at the end of that journey, over the horizon, lies the life you want to live.

As you look at this road, at that horizon, you have two choices:

You can stay where you are, living a life that is not truly the life you want for yourself, your family, and your future. You can sit there, imagining every possible roadblock, alternate route, hairpin turn, deer running unexpectedly across the road, that might lie on the journey ahead. You can think, "Well, it's probably better just to stay here."

Or you can set off down that road. You can embark on that journey. You can set the most outlandish destination, the most shoot-for-the-stars life you want to live—and get there sooner than you ever thought possible.

It sounds like an easy choice to make, right? But many people—including myself, at one point in my life—are still stuck not living the life they want. After all, starting this journey can be intimidating. Where do you even want to go? What is even possible? How do you know what lies ahead? How do you know what curves or obstacles are coming? How can you be sure you won't careen off the road into a horrible, fiery crash?

This mindset might seem reasonable, but it is rooted in fear—and when you are rooted in fear, it can be very difficult—even impossible—to reach that horizon. Well, I have good news: you don't have to start this journey and follow the road alone. You can have a whole team at your back and a whole community of like-minded travelers by your side to help you throughout your whole journey so you can live the life you want for you, your family, and your future.

That is what we do at Invst. Invst and the Invst4Life™ operating system were born out of a passion for helping people live the life they want to live. Our mission is to help educate, guide, and counsel people so they can reach their full financial potential. The Invst4Life™ operating system allows you to achieve financial freedom by building and owning your personal economy, which enables you to adapt to financial changes like market volatility, life events, sickness, death, disability and other economic conditions that are out of your control. Invst4Life™ is a values-based approach to total financial life management, centered in a belief that mindset is more important than money in achieving your full financial potential. Invst4Life™ changes the wealth management game to make money work for you. It is a movement of people living the lives they want to live, with full financial freedom, for themselves, their families, and their futures.

At the heart of the Invst4Life™ operating system are six core principles that will help you reach financial freedom faster: the Freedom Wheel™:

The Freedom Wheel™ is a visual illustration of the Invst4Life™ process made up of proven principles designed around you, your family, and your future. Through the Freedom Wheel™, you can establish your *Why* for money, get the right people on your team, organize all your financial information into a Financial Gameboard™, create a

Financial Life Scorecard™ to measure your success, establish rules based off your InvstDNA™, work off a model that adjusts and adapts to life, and discover the power of getting one dollar to do multiple things.

In my last book, *#FutureHack!*, I shared ten steps to hack your financial future and reach your full financial potential. In this book, you'll see how those hacks become part of a comprehensive, holistic financial process and mindset. You'll explore the simple secrets the wealthy have lived by that you can apply to your future today. You'll dive into each of the six principles of the Freedom Wheel—*Why*, *Who*, *Gameboard*, *Rules*, *Execution*, and *Acceleration*. You'll learn how and why they work, how they interact with each other to create a comprehensive financial model, how you can implement them in your financial life, and how they can take you across the finish line to financial freedom and the life you want to live faster than you ever thought possible. Finally, you'll see how all of these principles tie together in the Invst4Life™ process—a financial program that grows and evolves as you, your family, and your dreams do.

This is a book for people who love their families and who want simple solutions—and what you will read here is unlike anything else you will find in the financial services world. No other company does what Invst does, because no other company is built around principles the way Invst is. No other company has their philosophies ingrained into their process the way Invst does. What Invst does simply does not exist anywhere else.

Because at Invst, the principles of the Freedom Wheel™ and the Invst4Life™ process are not just concepts. They are not hypothetical structures we believe work in theory. They constitute an actual strategy that we *know* works—because we have the proof.

We have worked with thousands of people over the past 20 years, and out of that experience, we have built this system, this program, this process, this movement, that we *know* will work for you, your family, and your future. We have helped thousands of people on their journeys, collecting tens of thousands of ideas and experiences. We've cracked the code to help you reach financial freedom faster, to become work optional faster, to protect yourself in all areas so you can be free from worry, enabling you to live the life you want to live.

And we *know* it works because we implement it with our clients every single day and see how it allows them to accelerate to the life they want to live. The advice and solutions we render to our clients not only meet the highest degree of professional standards—they are also the same advice and services we would render to ourselves and our families.

Everything Invst has done for the past 20 years has led to this: delivering a solution to you, so you can begin your journey, today.

Invst is about mindset, and it is also about an actual, practical, actionable path you can follow to grow and protect your wealth—and the opportunity to learn from and work with the very advisors who put these principles into action every day and connect with thousands of others who are on their own journey to financial freedom.

Because Invst is more than just a process. Invst is a philosophy, a movement, a community. You are not alone—we are all on this journey together. When you start this journey, you've got not just all of us at Invst, but everyone who is part of the Invst movement alongside you.

Traditional financial thinking has limited people for far too long. It has slowed the progress of so many toward achieving their full financial potential. It's time to redefine your personal economy so you can be financially free to live the life you want to live under your own terms and conditions. It's *your* life, *your* family, *your* future. It's *your* journey. It's *your* story. It's the life *you* want to live. Invst is the vehicle, the process, the movement, that will get you there faster. The life you want is just beyond the horizon—why wait? Why not get there sooner?

If you are ready to join the movement, if you are ready to begin your journey, if you are ready to start accelerating toward the life you want—let's get started!

1

What's Stopping You From Accelerating?

Reaching financial freedom isn't about how much money you have or don't have. It's about living the life you love.

—Scott Jarred

When it comes to money, four things can happen in your life:

1. You can live with money.
2. You can die with money.
3. You can live without money.
4. You can die without money.

If I asked which one of these scenarios is most frightening to you, what would you answer? If you said, "Living without money," you have the same answer as 98 percent of the world. They say money can't buy happiness—I don't know about you, but I'd rather try to figure out happiness *with* money than without it.

Almost half of all families today report the number one source of stress in their life is their financial situation and decisions related to finances. That stress has led to a multiple year trend of more people filing for bankruptcy than divorce—and the one often leads to the other. As of January 2023, 60 percent of American adults live paycheck to paycheck.[1] Less than 50 percent have more than three months of savings at hand at any given time.[2] 42 percent have less than $1000 in savings.[3] 47 percent of older Americans have less than $50,000 saved for retirement,[4] and 32 percent don't have a single dime saved for retirement.[5] A full 40 percent of retired Americans are living on Social Security alone.[6]

Despite these dire statistics, startlingly few people do anything to really improve their financial lives. Most people stay right where they are, rather than starting the journey toward financial freedom and accelerating to the life they want to live.

I don't share this information to scare you, but to awaken you. As we all know, history is doomed to repeat itself unless intentional action is taken. The time for that action is now—and the person who can take action is you, reading this.

If:

- you feel overwhelmed by whether you will ever get to a point where you can be work optional and live a life on your own terms,
- you agree it is harder to keep what you make with increases in taxes, standards of living, helping the ones you love and the ever-increasing costs of goods and services,

- you aren't sure what sources of information to use to make your financial decisions,
- you lack the time and patience to know if you are making the right financial decisions in today's fast-paced, ever-changing environment,
- all of this is leading you to keep your foot on the brake, living in scarcity and uncertainty instead of accelerating toward financial freedom,

YOU ARE NOT ALONE. At Invst, we're here to make sure you are not part of any of those statistics. If living without money is your greatest fear, we're here to make sure that never becomes a reality.

How can you feel confident enough to start your journey? It starts with a simple shift in mindset: understanding that *you can do this*.

Adjust Your Mindset

A prospective client came in recently who has quite a bit of money sitting in cash. He completely cashed out of all his investment positions because of the current market volatility, meaning he probably sold at the bottom of the market. He is 100 percent fearful of the future. He's paying down his three percent, 30-year fixed mortgage at an accelerated rate because he has no better way to make his money work for him. He's overfunding his savings account because he's afraid of the market. Instead of buying low and selling high he's buying high and selling low. He's anxious about how his money is flowing. He's afraid of the unknown. And he is completely unaware that his income is not protected and his family would not be secure if something happened to him. He doesn't realize he's one car accident away from losing all his assets because of improper liability protection. He's not confident in his strategies, and I can see why: in his current position he has zero chance of building enough wealth to replace his current income in the future. And his fear is costing him millions of dollars of future lost wealth from which he will never be able to recover.

He's frozen, stuck where he is, doing the complete opposite of what smart money does in these times. He's in the accumulation phase of his life, when he should be accelerating, but instead he is living a life of scarcity, trying to navigate all the unknowns. Instead of going forward, he is stuck where he is—and is definitely not accelerating toward having his money work for him and his bigger future.

He's not living the life he wants because he doesn't know what to do. He's stuck because he's afraid of rolling back downhill, when in fact he should be confidently accelerating to make it up over the hill to the life he wants. When you're in a valley with a hill in front of you, you can't just sit there. If you do, your momentum will be completely stopped. You can't make irrational decisions in a valley simply because you can't see what's on the other side of the hill. You need to confidently accelerate up the hill knowing you are on the right path. And when you're on the hill, in the accumulation phase of your life, you can't just stay where you are, not moving forward. If you don't embark on that journey, you'll never make it to the top.

It's the decisions you make and actions you take in the valleys of life that will take you to living the life you want.

Successful people create success when they make the right decisions in the valley. The valley is where you win the game of life. It's what you do in those times that make or break you. It's easy at the top—the peaks are the fun part! It's the decisions you make and actions you take in the valleys of life that will take you to living the life you want. *Accelerate* will teach you the key principles you will need to carry you through the valleys of life.

All of this fear and hesitation is a symptom of a scarcity mindset—something I talked about in my previous book, *#FutureHack*. (If you don't have a copy, get your free one here: FutureHackMyLife.com/free-book-order, or scan the QR code below!)

A hack is a simple solution to a common problem, and the common problem is moving out of scarcity to abundance.

A scarcity mindset says there isn't enough to go around. It gives the illusion you can't afford to make those small daily choices that inch you closer to success—so you eventually settle instead of living the life you want.

A scarcity mindset makes you think, "I can't do that." The opposite of a scarcity mindset is an abundance mindset, which says, "How *can* I do that?" An abundance mindset believes you can accomplish anything you want by putting your resources to work for you. An abundance mindset views every situation you encounter as an opportunity for success. An abundance mindset knows if you continue to make the right choices every day, you will achieve your most ambitious dreams—and more.

With an abundance mindset, you can do more than just survive—you can thrive. You can create environments that foster your most important goals and turn your dreams into reality. You can become the CEO and Visionary of your total financial life, putting yourself in a position of control over your own destiny. You can have the confidence to know your future will be amazing—because *you* wrote it, which will allow you to accelerate toward financial freedom faster than you ever thought possible.

Reaching financial freedom isn't about how much money you have or don't have. We all have the same potential—success isn't prescribed only to a select few. The difference is those who pursue the life they want understand success takes what it takes. They understand the way they think about their everyday actions and choices makes all the difference.

Understand the Challenges

Even with an abundance mindset, there are still certain challenges to building wealth—challenges that can make you feel like you're just spinning your wheels, stuck in the valley of life. You're working harder and harder just to achieve the same results—like trying to accelerate when your car is in neutral and wondering why you're not getting anywhere.

I recently drove my daughter's Jeep to the lake to pull our jet skis out of the water. The Jeep was at the water at the end of the boat ramp, and the jet skis were all hooked up. I hit the gas—and it went nowhere. The Jeep wouldn't go. Every time I took my foot off the gas pedal, I would slide back further toward the water. I was about to sink my daughter's Jeep—with me in it. Then I realized: the car wouldn't move forward with the tow unless it had four-wheel drive activated. In order to get the car and the jet skis out of the water, I had to be very intentional about when it was time to shift into four-wheel drive, accelerate, and move forward. If I sat idle, the car—and I—would end up underwater. I had to understand the rules and make a change to how I was driving.

It's scary to have your foot on the gas and not move forward. It's scary to feel like if you make one mistake, your financial life will slide backward into the water and sink down with you in it. It's scary to not know why you can't seem to get ahead—why your journey doesn't seem to be getting you closer to the life you want.

The fact is, when it comes to money, it's not what you make that's important—it's what you keep. If your goal is to build up money so you can retire someday and have an income for your family, but you are just sitting on your money, then your money is not working as hard as you are. In fact, it is actively eroding. There are outside elements affecting your money 24 hours a day, seven days a week, 365 days a year: inflation, lawsuits, planned obsolescence, taxes, unexpected life events, fees and consumer financing, changes in technology, increased standard of living, law changes, wear and tear, market fluctuations, and more.

Understanding the factors eroding your money and what to do about them is critical to building wealth. You can make all the money in the world, but if you lose it to those eroding factors, you still won't build wealth. In the over 2,500 households we've worked with, we have found there are four main challenges to building wealth. The details of each individual situation differ, but the challenge always falls into one—or more—of these categories:

- Lost opportunity cost
- Rules of financial institutions

- Velocity of money
- Lack of organization and coordination

I talk about all of these in more detail in *#FutureHack!*, but I'll share a brief summary of each of them here.

Lost Opportunity Cost

I guarantee you: money is leaking out of your life, and you don't even know it. Most people lose five to ten percent of every dollar they put in their pocket—to financial institutions, taxes, poor choice of fixed expenditures such as paying for your debt, or just not doing anything with that money and letting it sit stagnant. It's like a leak in your engine you don't know about: you keep filling up your gas tank, and the next day the tank is empty again, even though all you did was commute to work and back.

Lost opportunity cost is the money you lose as the result of any particular financial decision versus another. Not only does it consider the present value that was lost, but also the future value that is lost. If you pay $1,500 in taxes on an investment, not only do you lose $1,500, but also what that $1,500 would be worth in the future if it was in that same investment.

Say you are getting a new car. If you lease the car, you can write off the expenses as a business. If you buy the car, you can depreciate it. How do you weigh and measure the tax savings and the lost opportunity cost of one versus the other? Taking into account interest rates and having a car payment, what is the byproduct lost opportunity of that decision? What's the lost opportunity of an investment return that could have accumulated in a tax-deferred account?

Because it's not just the money you lose one time—it's the compound effect. You have to take the money you lost at the next best rate of return and look at what it would be over a 10-, 20-, or 30-year period. For example, if you lost one dollar today, what would that dollar have been worth in 10 or 20 years? If you were earning seven percent on it for 10 years, that one dollar would have grown to almost $20. So really, you lost $20. In thirty years, every dollar would be worth six times more!

Most people have no conception of all this lost money, and most financial plans are not effective in finding it. If you put one dollar in your pocket and a dime falls out, wouldn't you want to pick up that dime? Well, it's only a dime, so maybe not. But if you put $1,000 in your pocket and $100 fell out, you'd want to recapture that $100, wouldn't you? Most people would be chasing that $100 bill down the street to get it back!

With every decision about your money, your financial team should consider whether it will create a lost opportunity cost today or in the future—and have a plan to recapture lost money. This allows you to weigh and measure whether that lost opportunity cost is worth it, or whether it is better to recapture that dollar and put it back to work.

Every time you lose money, it's not just the money you lose, but the opportunity it could have given you.

Every time you lose money, it's not just the money you lose, but the opportunity it could have given you. One dollar today is worth six times that in 30 years—so really, you've lost the opportunity to grow your money six times over.

If you look at your full financial picture, I guarantee you could find five to ten percent of your money falling out of your proverbial pocket. By looking at the big picture, you could recapture that five to ten percent and put it back to work. As shocking as this might sound, this alone can create two to five million dollars' worth of spendable wealth in your lifetime!

But that depends on what you do with the lost money when you find it. Most people, if they find that lost opportunity cost, decide it's easier not to make a real decision about what to do with the money. Most of the time it just gets spent and not put to work for you. It could be sitting in a financial institution (i.e., bank) working for the bank, not you. Not making a decision is a lost opportunity cost as well—because financial institutions themselves present a challenge to building wealth.

The Rules of Financial Institutions

When you place money inside a financial institution, you have to understand the rules financial institutions follow. The agendas of financial institutions are very simple:

1. They want your money.
2. They want it systematically.
3. They want to hold on to it as long as possible.
4. They want to give you back as little as possible when the time comes.

Every product financial institutions offer is designed with those intents.

401(k)s are a perfect example. For years, employers have provided employees with 401(k)s. Most of us have one and see it as part of our full financial retirement planning. The financial institution wants your money, and they get it in the form of your contributions to your 401(k). They want it systematically—i.e. coming out of every paycheck. They want to hold onto it as long as possible—until you are 59 ½ years old. And if you want that money back, there are consequences: if you want to get it back early, you have to pay a penalty. If you want it back after you turn 59 ½, you'll pay long-term taxes or even higher taxes later. And for all that time, instead of working for you, that money is working for the financial institution.

The rules of financial institutions are not built to empower you. They are not built to help you win—they are built to help the financial institutions you work with win. But knowing these simple rules can help you make different decisions that can free up new money so you can use your money the way you want, rather than succumbing to the agendas of financial institutions.

In fact, you can learn how to manage your money the way banks do. You can take your money and put it to work doing what *you* want it to do, not what somebody else has planned for it. As a consumer, why are your dollars only doing one thing? Why aren't your dollars doing multiple things, the way they do at banks? How do you create more benefits and money supply with one dollar, like a bank does?

That is the next challenge: how to get your dollars to do more than one thing by multiplying your money using the concept of the velocity of money.

Velocity of Money

What financial institutions understand, and what individuals often fail to understand, is that every dollar can accomplish more than one thing at a time.

Say you take $100 to your local bank. When you put that money into the bank, the bank doesn't take that $100 and stick it into a big metal safe like you see in the movies. What they actually do is take those hundred dollars, go to the Federal Reserve, and for a small interest payment (which the bank marks up for you so they can keep the spread), the bank gets a thousand dollars back from the Federal Reserve for that money—ten times its value. Then, they loan those thousand dollars out—not just once, but multiple times.

If you go to the bank for a student loan, they charge you interest. If you go to that same bank for a mortgage, they charge you interest. If you go to that same bank for a credit card, they charge you interest. If you go to that bank for a loan for a new car, they charge you interest. All of those loans come from that same $1000 they got for your $100 (plus the many thousands they got from many other people's $100). The $100 you put into that bank has now been given back to you many times over—and you're paying a small spread on that $100 each time.

What if you could put yourself in the middle? What if *you* could be the bank? Rather than giving financial institutions money and letting them leverage it for multiple spreads, what if you could teach your dollar to do multiple things and create small spreads along the way? That is the velocity of money—the exponential power of what money can do.

It takes money to make money—or rather, it takes the movement of money to make money. That's why you need a team of financial advisors working together to make sure your dollars are creating money even while you sleep.

Lack of Organization

All three of these challenges are united under the overarching theme of the fourth challenge: lack of financial organization and coordination.

Organization and coordination are essential for success. Lack of organization is a major reason why people lose. The Vanderbilts were once one of the richest families in the world—but they didn't have their finances organized and coordinated, and they ended up losing all their money. If none of the various systems in your car are communicating with each other, how do you expect that vehicle to function to get you where you want to go?

Let me ask you some questions:

- Are all your finances organized in one place?
- Could you access all of your most important documents, see your current net worth statements, your personal Profit and Loss statements, all updating in real time, on your phone or computer, right now?
- Do you know how all the pieces of your financial life interact with and complement one another?

If your answer is no, you are not alone. When it comes to their financial life, most people have no overarching organization, no rules, and no financial beliefs they live by. They have multiple products that were purchased with no real idea of how they work, multiple different advisors handling different aspects of their financial life, and no rhyme or reason to how any of these elements correlate with each other. It's just a hodgepodge of decisions all thrown together.

Trying to create a successful financial future out of a financial junk drawer is like trying to play chess without knowing the rules—and without a gameboard.

Trying to create a successful financial future out of this is like trying to play a game of chess without understanding the rules and how each piece works: your chances of winning the game are next to none—especially when you don't even have a gameboard.

The Financial Junk Drawer

We call this common syndrome the financial junk drawer. The financial junk drawer is a composite of all the financial decisions you've made in your lifetime. It's a drawer—metaphorical but often literal as well—that every financial decision you've ever made (plus the statements that come along with those decisions) goes into. Like a junk drawer, there is no coordination or integration of those products, decisions, relationships, and statements. There is no one place you can go and see everything all at one time laid out in an organized way.

When it comes time to deal with finances or make a financial decision, you pull open that drawer and try to lay everything out on the kitchen table. But your kitchen table isn't a gameboard. It hasn't been set up to play the game. It doesn't have any rules outlined. There is no way to really see how all the pieces relate to, interact with, and affect each other, so there is no way to make a holistic financial decision. And God forbid you pass away and leave your family to try and sort out that junk drawer—we've seen that happen far too often.

A financial junk drawer can paralyze you. When you reach the point of needing to make a financial decision, you don't have the information you need at hand. All you have is chaos. When your mind is chaotic and unorganized, you tend to make decisions based on emotion, rather than rules and evidence. You don't have the data to weigh and measure your decisions, so you start listening to whoever sounds best in the moment—whether it's Dave Ramsey or your insurance provider or your coworker at the water cooler who heard about this cool new product you should try. You make an uninformed, emotional decision without understanding the ripple effect on your wealth.

Without organization and coordination, people make financial decisions in a vacuum. Often, you'll have a financial advisor making a decision on your behalf who doesn't understand the entirety of your financial situation. They make decisions in a microeconomic way that impacts their little microeconomic slice of your financial life—but those decisions can have a ripple effect through your entire macroeconomic life. It could be as simple as what kind of mortgage you get, and yet it could deeply impact your wealth, your tax benefits, and many other areas of your financial life.

Understanding all the pieces and how they move is critical to understanding your financial situation—but it's not your fault if you don't have it all clearly laid out. It's not how we are trained to handle our finances or how finances function in America. The average person interacts with 13 financial institutions at any given moment in their life—and often with many hundreds of financial institutions over their lifetime—and each one of those institutions has their own agenda for your money. They're each tugging your dollar in a different direction. Someone from one financial institution is going to give different advice than someone from another financial institution—which will be different from the advice you get from your coworker at the watercooler or from a talking head on the news.

This is why people often find themselves in the middle of their financial life with 13 advisors around them giving instructions—but those 13 advisors have never sat down at a table together and had a conversation about what you want from your money, what you are trying to accomplish, what journey you are on, what you want your life to be.

With organization and coordination, with a gameboard that lays out all the pieces of your financial life and how they connect to and affect each other, all of those microeconomic decisions can be made with a full understanding of their impact on the macroeconomic picture.

You can't win the game of wealth building and own your Personal Economy without an organized, rules-based financial model that helps you evaluate the collective whole. Without organization and coordination, you may be leaking money. With organization and coordination, you can recapture that money. Without organization and coordination, you won't be able to see if a piece is missing, and you'll always have a nagging worry in the back of your mind. When you know that everything is organized and aligned, you don't have to worry about missing pieces. You can have peace of mind and harmony.

Awareness

Not being cognizant of these challenges is like being on a journey and wandering off course without even realizing it. You're getting further from your destination, from the life you want to live, using up your resources, and you can't see where you are going in order to course correct. All these challenges are detrimental—maybe not today, but tomorrow, next week, next month, next year, in five years. But you don't know it until you come to an important decision, a fork in the road—and by then you are totally lost, miles away from where you want to be, with countless obstacles blocking your path back. Once you are aware of these challenges, you can make a plan and develop strategies and processes to remove or avoid those obstacles—or even use them to your advantage.

On an open road with no obstacles, you can accelerate as fast as you want, your journey a clear, straight line to the life you want. Unfortunately, the road of life is never entirely straight and clear. There will always be obstacles that arise—and these four challenges (1. Rules of financial institutions; 2. Velocity of money; 3. Lack of organization; 4. Lost opportunity cost) in particular will never disappear from reality. But if you are cognizant of them, you can maneuver more quickly because you know how to make the right decisions—for your present and for your future.

Know Where You're Going

If you don't know where you are going, if you don't know where your journey leads, if you don't know what future you are trying to reach, you can't accelerate toward it. Without a destination, you have no way of knowing which paths will get you there fastest, which obstacles will throw you off course, which turns will send you out of your way and delay your arrival at the life you want to live.

In order to know where your journey leads, you have to determine what financial freedom means to you.

When we ask clients what financial freedom means to them, we hear many different answers—but over the years, out of thousands of conversations with people from all walks of life, we have found they all come down to Four Freedoms: freedom of money, freedom of time, freedom of relationships, and freedom of purpose. Dan Sullivan astutely outlined these Four Freedoms™ in relation to entrepreneurialism,[7] but they are equally true for individuals. In every way, shape or form, everything you are fighting for almost certainly fits into one of these categories.

Often, people will say, "I just don't want to have to work forever. I want to be work optional." That is freedom of time. But you can't get freedom of time without freedom of money. Without money, you don't really have control of your time, because you have to work to earn an income. Freedom of money means being able to generate the cash flow required for you to be able to spend your time doing the things you enjoy.

Once you have freedom of money and freedom of time, who do you want to spend it with? Perhaps you want to spend it with your spouse or your children and grandkids or your best friends. That is freedom of relationships.

And finally, once you have that time, what do you truly want to do? What gives you joy, what fulfills you, what gives you purpose? Instead of spending all your time and energy working on something you're not passionate about just to pay the bills, you can do what truly gives meaning to your life. That is freedom of purpose.

What is *Your* Freedom?

These are the basic tenets of financial freedom. Now, you just need to plug in the specifics of what they mean for you and your financial world. What purpose does money serve in your life? Sure, it allows you to buy things, but think deeper than that. What does money truly enable you to do?

These are the values that money helps you fulfill. These questions are the building blocks of your personal philosophy. That philosophy will dictate how you are going to approach your financial life, and it will change your entire view of what living the life you want can truly mean—and how the financial decisions you make can turn those dreams into reality.

Once you articulate what you are fighting for, what freedom means specifically for you, then you can start putting the financial side into place behind it. You can determine what financial success means to you. You can articulate, if we were sitting here three years from now, what would need to happen for you to feel financially successful, what dramatic impacts on your life you would need to see.

No one can tell you what to believe. You have to decide that for yourself. Invst is simply here to help you discover your "why" behind money, to help you craft your individual philosophy and in turn facilitate effective action to fulfill that philosophy. Our goal is to give you the pen and let you design the life you want to live, design what financial freedom looks like for you, design your own story, journey, and destiny. Our job is to help educate, guide and counsel you on that journey so you can accelerate to the life you want for yourself, your family, and your future.

When you know where you are going, when you know where the road leads, you can tell whether or not you are on track, whether or not you are moving in the right direction. For the first time in your life, you can now pre-set your financial GPS and know exactly where you are going. And once you have that road before you, once you know what's over the horizon, once you know what obstacles may lie in your way and how to avoid them, once you have your mind set to abundance, there's no reason to waste more time living a life that is not the life you want. It's time to accelerate toward owning your personal economy.

What does accelerating actually look like? Well, to start with, you need a strategy that can handle the journey ahead. At Invst, the heart of that strategy is The Freedom Wheel™.

2

Six Principles for Freedom

The only constant in life is change. Accelerating means always changing and evolving for the better, always leveling up, always grateful for what you had in the past and always moving forward toward your bigger future.

—Scott Jarred

If you are staring down a winding road, not knowing what lies ahead, not knowing where you are going, of course the idea of setting out on a journey down that road is scary. But what if you could plot out the path you are on, know where it ends, *and* be prepared for the inevitable changes, unexpected obstacles, personal growth and evolution you'll find along the way? What if you could secure your ability to live the life you want to live—and confidently accelerate to get there faster?

The first step of any journey begins with a decision—so how you make decisions is the first thing you need to understand.

How Do You Make Financial Decisions?

Generally speaking, there are five ways people make financial decisions.

Day-to-Day

Day-to-day decision making involves no planning. Instead, you are just moving through life: getting up, going to work, coming home, resetting and doing it again, over and over. You've never given any intentional thought to your future, what you want it to be and how you are going to get there. You are flying by the seat of your pants, making decisions off the cuff in the moment, on a whim. Your financial decisions are dependent on what money is in the bank at the end of the day or the end of the month. That is how you determine your future.

This is how a solid majority of people live. Each day they say, "I'll go invest in this." "I'll open this account." "I'll pay for this purchase this way." "I got paid today, so I'm going to make this purchase."

The results of day-to-day planning can be devastating. People who don't plan tend to live day by day and may lose control of their financial lives. They become vulnerable to the events and circumstances that surround them. In a complex

In a complex society such as ours, people who do not plan have less chance for financial security and the peace of mind it brings.

society such as ours, people who do not plan have less chance for financial security and the peace of mind it brings.

Event-Based

Event-based decision making is how many people make decisions. This type of decision-making usually keeps people one step behind where they could and should be. Maybe you occasionally sit down and put a budget together. Maybe you occasionally meet with a financial professional or CPA for certain circumstances. When something pops up, you make a decision about it. Your employer offers a 401(k), so you say, "Oh, I guess I'll sign up for that." This is a long-term decision, but you still make it on the fly without thinking it through—even though it may have a big impact on your life and your future.

Event-based decision making often involves making a decision based on what you feel at that time—because someone else is doing it, or because you heard someone talking about it on TV—but without any real thought going into it. You see a stock tip online, so you decide to make a buy. You feel bad that day because of something happening in the world—such as Covid, or a new president taking office—so you make emotional decisions based on a feeling. There's no strategy for how those decisions connect to anything else. You're making choices without really knowing how it will impact you, whether it will benefit you or harm you down the road.

Event-based decision making is also part of the do-it-yourself mindset. Many people do not understand the importance of having professional assistance given on a timely basis. Instead, they rely on the myriad do-it-yourself financial tools out there, setting up their finances without fully understanding what they are doing and often doing more harm than good.

Because of all this, event-based decision makers almost never reach their full financial potential—or full financial freedom.

Needs-Based

Needs-based decision-making focuses on meeting specific needs such as saving for a house, college tuition costs, retirement income, paying estate taxes, disability income needs, etc. This kind of decision-making usually takes place only when the need is present or obvious. It is reactive versus proactive. You only think about it when the need arises—maybe a bit in advance, but not anticipating and planning for it far in advance.

Needs-based planning tries to predict the needs you'll have in the future—but the future is not certain, and often your predictions will fall short of the actual optimal need, even for simple things like how much you'll need to pay off your house, how much you'll need to send your kid to college, how much you'll need to live on when you retire. Those guesstimates change as your life circumstances change—but you don't necessarily update your financial plans to reflect those changes.

Traditional Planning

For those who do commit to some kind of financial planning, this is the most common type in today's world: you sit with a planner, they find multiple needs, they line up a map of ideas, and try to fulfill those ideas with the isolated products they carry through the financial institutions they represent.

Traditional financial planning focuses on meeting predetermined needs and goals. The methodology used in financial planning often involves number crunching and monitoring of mathematical variables such as interest rates, investment rates of return, inflation rates, tax rates and future income needs. Financial planning focuses on how much additional money is required to obtain a predetermined need or goal by using this formula: Wealth = Money x Rate x Time

Traditional financial planning is a very linear approach to what will happen in the future. It mostly assumes the world never changes, and that everything is in a perfect linear format. A traditional financial plan is like driving a car that has the accelerator set to 55 miles per hour all the time. You can't go slower, you can't go faster, you can't adjust to the circumstances that arise.

If the road is a perfectly straight road, with no obstacles or unexpected turns, no boulders or potholes or animals crossing, and you have perfect weather the whole way, then this would work great. But we all know life is anything but linear. The road of life is never straight.

This is why traditional financial planning can fail: it cannot withstand the unexpected—and it doesn't address those eroding factors we talked about last chapter. Because of that, most of these plans fall woefully short of getting you to financial freedom—and are often abandoned midstream because of their ineffectiveness.

Financial Positioning

The alternative to financial planning is financial positioning—creating a financial *model*, rather than a financial *plan*. Financial positioning makes sure you are organized and positioned so when something unexpected happens, when that deer runs across the road or there's an unexpected tree blocking your way, you are able to react and make an adjustment so you don't get thrown off course. You are always in the right position, and you can now own your personal economy.

The Invst4Life™ process focuses on helping you discover your true why for money and educating you on how to think abundantly, well beyond needs, toward reaching financial freedom. This process puts you in the driver's seat of your journey, with your money working for you instead of others. It focuses on efficient and effective ways to build wealth, allowing you to adapt to constant change and protecting you against the unforeseen, such as taxes, inflation, market fluctuations and claims from creditors.

Rather than creating a long-form report that says, "Here is your life for the next 30 years," this process provides daily optimization: finding lost money, making sure you control your controllables with protection and risk management, using a gameboard to keep everything organized. That way, if you get sick, if the market crashes, if your house is damaged in a flood, if there's a recession, if there's a global pandemic—you always know what to do. No matter what happens during your journey, you are still always accelerating toward the life you want to live.

There is only one constant in life: Change. Your ability to effectively react to change is a key determinant in your success. A financial model, rather than a set financial plan, allows you to adapt to change—but it's about more than that. For the first time, this is about you: putting you in a position of power and control over your financial life and making sure your money is aligned with the values and decisions you want to make for the life you want to live.

How is this done? By having a set of principles that enable you to make the right decision so you can continue moving forward on your journey, rather than standing still because you have no idea what to do.

The Importance of Principles

Having principles is the best way to get the peace of mind and harmony you deserve while simultaneously building your value and wealth. Anyone who has found success has some set of principles that help them on their journey, that help them stay on track and grow. If you look at any really successful system or philosophy out there, it is built on a set of principles that grow and evolve but stand the course of time.

Ray Dalio wrote a book called *Principles*, in which he outlines the principles he's used to become one of the richest men in the world. He's one of the most successful investors of all time, the owner of the very successful company Bridgewater Associates, which has a team of brilliant people working together to create extraordinary value for their clients. He was able to accomplish all this because he had principles which were the framework of everything he did to build his company.

Warren Buffett has a series of principles he lives by today. If you go into his office, he has newspaper articles from bad times up on his walls to remind him of what life could be like, so he doesn't forget the past and deviate from his principles. Nick Saban, widely considered one of the greatest coaches in college football history, has a set of principles and a game book that allows everyone in the organization to do what they need to do without him having to micromanage everyone on a day-in, day-out basis. The great American businessman Jack Welch wrote books on managing a business using principles and rules.

Successful businesses with great leaders, successful sports teams with great coaches—they all have rule books, goals, visions for their companies or teams. They all have playbooks with underlying principles that guide them to success. But there has never been a real playbook for normal people who are trying to find personal financial success.

A business exists to do one thing, which makes it easier to create a set of principles designed to help that business accomplish that one thing. Those principles can help the business run for a century without changing. But a person's life, and a family's life, changes. There are seasons within one's life. That's why you need a set of principles that can always be your foundation through all those seasons, that can evolve with you and your family, and your different goals and needs in those different seasons.

What Are Principles?

As you move through your life journey, you grow and change, your circumstances grow and change, the world grows and changes. Principles are the things that can stand the test of time because they grow and change with you while providing a fundamental, solid foundation to build on. Accelerating means being on a journey of progress in which you are always getting better, always leveling up, always grateful for what you had in the past, and always moving forward toward the future. Principles allow you to continue to evolve along the way.

Principles are the things that can stand the test of time because they grow and change with you while providing a fundamental, solid foundation to build on.

Principles provide a foundation you can go back to for every single financial decision. Every time your circumstances change, you don't have to wonder what to do, because the principles will always be with you to hold you up. If you have principles, if you have rules for your money, you're not always second guessing yourself, or trying to time the market, trying to figure out when to get in and when to get out. You're not worrying about what to do with your money, because it's already pre-programmed.

We all come in contact with different situations, different messes in our lives, and how we accelerate through them will differ. But with the tools, resources, and principles in place to make decisions, you'll be able to accelerate correctly and appropriately. When you have that structure in place, you'll have less anxiety about your finances because you know that every dollar is programmed to go to work, and every part of your financial life will be operating the way it should.

Knowing is always better than just thinking and feeling. When you make decisions based on what you feel or think, you are often letting yourself be ruled by emotions or whatever the flavor of the day is. When you make a decision based on what you *know*, that decision is based on evidence, data, and facts. If you rely only on thinking and feeling, you will likely find your journey stalled. If you rely on what you *know*, you can progress on your journey with confidence. With the right principles, no matter what the weather is, no matter what the road conditions are, you can accelerate forward.

Fundamentally, there are six principles you need to accelerate your journey to financial freedom and the life you want to live. They are the six principles that make up the Freedom Wheel™.

The Freedom Wheel™

The six principles of the Freedom Wheel™ are what give you the freedom to accelerate your journey, knowing you are heading in the right direction, toward the life you want to live. Each principle builds on the others, and it all revolves around you, your family, and your future.

Why: Your *Why* for money is more important than money itself. Once you know your true "why" for money, you can put rules, evidence, and strategies in place, which allows you to build a model that can adapt and overcome any financial situation in order to keep you on the path to live the life you want. Your future will be kind to you because you will write it.

Who: Who is accountable to help you get to your *Why*? A board of directors who coordinate, collaborate, and communicate on your behalf. Each of those directors needs to be aligned to your *Why* and match your values.

Gameboard: Your Financial *Gameboard*™ creates one unified place to weigh and measure your ideas. It shows your present position, where you are on your journey, and allows you to weigh, measure, and think four dimensionally about all your decisions, understanding both the short and long-term effects.

When these three principles are aligned, you'll have true financial peace of mind and harmony. If you know why you are doing something, you can find the people who will align with that *Why* to help you get there. If you have all your financial information together, those people will actually be able to see what's going on. Your financial junk drawer is organized—you don't need to make decisions in a vacuum. You know what pieces are on your *Gameboard* and who can help you move them properly in a coordinated fashion. You have the data and information to give to your *Who* so they can simulate where you want to go. And, most importantly, you *know* where you want to go—you know your *Why*.

Out of that peace of mind and harmony, you can then build your value and wealth. Each of these peace of mind and harmony principles correlates to a principle that builds value and wealth.

Rules: Your Rules tell your *Who*s what to do. If you don't have rules, someone else (like a financial institution) will create them for you. Ray Dalio, Warren Buffet, and all of the most successful financial minds of the world have a set of rules they have identified for themselves. Rules establish your InvstDNA™—your personal philosophy and belief about money, risk, and success. These rules are based on evidence, removing emotion and allowing for fact-based decisions.

Execution: Without execution, your vision for your future is merely a hallucination. *Execution* puts the pieces on your Financial *Gameboard*™ into action using a financial model that is ready to adapt and adjust to life's changes. This is where you have a personal financial accountability partner to help you achieve financial freedom.

Acceleration: Acceleration is the speed at which your money can replicate. To accelerate, you must remove scarcity and unlock opportunities so you can always live in a world of abundance. *Acceleration* means re-setting the levels in areas where you may have evolved and gotten better—including your *Why* and your vision for your life.

Your *Why* will evolve as you grow. The people around you will grow, and you may upgrade your *Who*, your board of directors, as you have different needs and goals. Your *Gameboard*, while it remains static, constantly has new information added. Your *Rules* can get clearer as you get more wisdom in your life. Your *Execution* will grow and shift to match where you are and where you are going as your journey progresses.

This is why it is important to set up a cadence of meetings and a Financial Life Scorecard™ to know if you are on track. You should continually check in on your journey and your destination, reevaluating and re-strategizing toward your future based on your present. Re-clarify your goals for the next year, for the next three years. Re-clarify your mission statement and see whether it has shifted.

Your future is going to be bigger and better than where you are now—so of course these principles will grow and evolve as you move toward that future. The Freedom Wheel™ is designed to be adaptable to whatever point you are at in your life because it is built for you and by you, for your family and by your family, for your future, and by your future. It constantly evolves, unlike a traditional financial plan where you just set it and forget it. This is a total financial life operating system.

If you follow these principles, you will be able to successfully navigate and accelerate appropriately through all the storms in your life. No matter what your journey in life is, these principles are going to help you get peace of mind and harmony. Peace of mind and harmony build value and wealth, and building value and wealth gives you peace of mind and harmony. The momentum of this keeps the Freedom Wheel™ turning, accelerating you faster and faster toward financial freedom and the life you want to live.

Putting the Wheel in Motion

The six principles of the Freedom Wheel™ power our financial process, Invst4Life™—and I am not being hyperbolic when I say there is nothing like it in the industry today.

Usually, people have a number of different financial processes to manage. Invst4Life™ has everything all interwoven together. Having one process that manages your entire financial life is unique. There are not many financial planning programs that look at every single aspect of your financial life holistically to determine whether they are optimized to help you achieve the life you want to live—and do so with principles that are built to support you, your family, and your future.

Invst4Life™ is the only financial planning process out there that actually creates a principles-based process, rather than selling a series of products. When institutions build processes, those processes tend to be for the purpose of pushing a product. Very rarely is there anything in the process on how to clearly design a principles-based decision system for yourself. If you go to Merrill Lynch, they will offer you an investment product, not a process. Same thing if you go to Northwestern Mutual for life insurance, or to your homeowner or auto insurance agent, or to your bank. Then you, as an individual, are stuck with how to weigh and measure whether that one product can help you. You don't own your personal economy—the institutions do.

Invst4Life™ doesn't push specific products. It follows six proven principles you can use to design the future you want—a framework that is built by you, for you.

Because of this, the Invst4Life™ process is not complex. It is simple and easy to follow. When you go through this process, you walk out with a Financial Life Scorecard™: a simple, streamlined document and web page that outlines your *Why*, your values, your mission statement, your Financial *Gameboard*™, your InvstDNA™, your *Whos*, your most important action items, your one-year goals, your 90 day actions, your opportunities, and dangers—all in one place that you can easily refer to and will help you make smarter decisions faster. This scorecard is then aggregated so that all financial decisions will be made using your electronic macroeconomic financial model, rather than making decisions based off hunches and guesswork. This allows you to make decisions smarter and quicker and also gives you the tools to help weigh and measure those decisions along the way.

And when you run across an obstacle, the process helps determine what the issue is and in what area it lies, and finds the specific, simple solution to fix it. It couldn't be more straightforward. Embedded throughout Invst4Life™ are 103 different hacks—specific tools—each designed to quickly and simply solve a specific financial issue. Anytime you have a problem, we place it where it goes on the Freedom Wheel™ and use a specific hack to fix it. (To learn more about these hacks, visit FutureHackMyLife.com!)

We know this process works because it's been battle tested. We have put it into practice for countless clients and seen them achieve tremendous success. Now, for the first time, you can have a total financial life operating system built on a solid foundation of principles that will help you run your family, run your life, give you peace of mind and harmony, and help you build value and wealth. And the best news is: you don't have to do it alone.

Your Personal CFO

If you are the CEO of your and your family's life, you should have a Personal CFO by your side on your journey.

A Personal CFO will lay out the gameboard for the game you want to play, make sure every piece on the gameboard is vetted, and set you up to win. Your Personal CFO helps you establish your most trusted board of advisors who are accountable and work collaboratively to help you live the life you want. Along the way, they will help you recapture those lost opportunity costs, harness the velocity of money, set your own rules instead of succumbing to the rules of financial institutions, help you craft and follow your rules, determine your InvstDNA™, align the data and evidence to create a strategy for your money to build value and generate multi-generational wealth.

Your Personal CFO sits next to you on your journey, giving you the confidence to accelerate. People end up stuck in lives that are not what they want because they aren't sure what to do. They aren't sure whether they should go for something. Instead of embarking on a journey, they stay where they are.

They don't have the answers. They don't know which way to go. With a Personal CFO, instead of staying stuck where you are, you can accelerate toward the life you want to live. They will be next to you, ready to help you through any twists and turns you might encounter along the way.

If you go visit the Indianapolis 500, you can take a ride in a tandem car. A professional racecar driver sits in the front seat, and you sit in the back seat—and you get to experience what it feels like to go around the racetrack at full racing speed. The driver goes full throttle the whole way—the pull of the Gs hitting the turns is unbelievable. I could never drive that fast around the track myself. But the driver has the experience and the skills to do it—and I get to experience the ride. Now I know what it feels like to drive the Indy 500!

Your Personal CFO will be that racecar driver—except you will be in the driver's seat, and your Personal CFO will be by your side showing you how to go. They have the expertise. They have the skills. They'll show you the true meaning of acceleration—and make sure you are safe and protected the whole time.

The Leader of the Journey

This is your financial life. No one else's. This means you have to lead the journey. Your job is to make the critical decisions in your own interest and to understand what is being done on your behalf. Your Personal CFO's job is to help you weigh and measure those decisions—to educate, guide, and counsel you toward reaching your full financial potential. They're here to provide you with the tools, education, and most importantly, the trusted partner you need to help navigate that journey.

Through the rest of this book, we will explore each of the six principles of the Freedom Wheel™ and see how they build on one another and fuel the Invst4Life™ process to give you the power to accelerate to financial freedom. You will learn how to accelerate your decision making by understanding yourself better, and how to accelerate your opportunities in life by removing dangers and enhancing your strengths. You will learn how to level up, how to reassess and accelerate, while continually scaling and growing, without worrying about the turns and obstacles and pitfalls on the road as you go through this journey.

Are you ready to hit the road?

3

WHY

Starting with "why" means defining your vision, purpose, beliefs, and values and using them to guide all of your decisions and actions. This will help you stay focused on what is most important for your life.

—Scott Jarred

Visionary Accelerators

Looking at the truly visionary accelerators throughout history, they all have one thing in common: they have been very clear about their mission—about their *Why*.

When you have a clear mission, it gives you direction and purpose, and it allows you to focus your energy and resources on achieving that goal. It also helps you attract like-minded individuals who share your passion and can help you achieve your mission.

John F. Kennedy's mission was to go to the moon. He didn't know how we were going to do it, but he stated that is what we, as a country, were going to accomplish. He increased NASA's budget by 89 percent, and NASA took us to the moon—because John F. Kennedy set that mission.

When you have a clear mission, it gives you direction and purpose, and it allows you to focus your energy and resources on achieving that goal.

Steve Jobs wanted to take the iPod and make it do everything. He wanted multiple devices to all be combined into one device that can do everything. He wanted to create technology that empowers people and enriches peoples' lives. That was his visionary mission.

Elon Musk wants to go to Mars. In order to get to Mars, he needed to start with Tesla, and he became the richest man in the world along the way. Walt Disney's mission for Disney World was to sell happiness, and he built "The Happiest Place On Earth."

Each of these visionaries said, "This is what I am going to do." My mission is the moon. My mission is Mars. My mission is to create a product that makes technology work for people. My mission is to sell happiness. They were all clear on their *Why*. They may not have known all the mechanics and logistics of how they were going to get to that destination—but they knew what the destination was.

It's also important to note that having a clear mission is just the starting point. These visionaries also surrounded themselves with the right people and created a system for making decisions and measuring progress. They had rules and principles they followed and used data, not emotion, to make decisions. They had a system for measuring and weighing their decisions in relation to how those decisions would advance them toward their goal, toward what they wanted to achieve. And they had to be adaptable and willing to adjust their approach as they encountered obstacles and challenges.

What's Your Family Mission?

Our families are no different. In order to truly accelerate on your journey toward the life you want to live, you need to know where you are headed. What is the goal for yourself, for your family? What do you want to achieve? Your personal mission might not be to get to Mars. It might simply be not to have to work all the time so you can spend more time with your family and travel the world with them. Maybe you want to be "work optional" in 10 years. Maybe you want to sell your business in 20 years.

Whatever your goal, it's the same process, the same journey, with the same questions: How do you make major decisions to achieve that goal? How do you put together a board of directors who can help you fulfill that mission? How do you create a gameboard and rules to execute that vision?

As you travel forward, your *Why* is what you are aiming for. It is where your journey is leading. If you don't know where your journey is leading, how are you going to know if you're heading the right way? How are you going to stay on track?

If you know what your goal is, you can accelerate toward it. All those visionary accelerators set visionary missions for themselves, and it gave them a clear destination. Without a vision, without a W*hy*, there is nothing to keep you heading in the right direction. Without a system of principles and rules built on a *Why*, you end up listening to the news or to what people are saying on social media and making decisions based on emotion, on the flavor of the day, rather than on facts, principles, and what is going to get you to your goal.

There is a reason Simon Sinek titled his groundbreaking book *Start With Why*. (If you haven't read it, I highly recommend it—that book was very instrumental in establishing the foundation at Invst to help people live the life they want!) Your *Why* is the destination you set in your GPS, the X at the end of the treasure map. If there's a road closure or an accident, if there's a storm or an obstacle in the way, you may need to reroute, but with that destination set, you will always be heading in the right direction.

A *Why* can be very simple yet very complex. Discovering your *Why* is crucial to having peace of mind and harmony for your life and your money. It is what will ultimately allow you to achieve financial freedom and the life you want to live.

The Formula for Success

The formula for financial success is very simple: success takes what it takes. Successful people do what unsuccessful people don't. They cultivate good habits and continue those good habits long after their financial success is realized. But while the formula may not change, we each have a different story to tell, because everyone's *Why* is different. Until you clearly understand what you believe in, you don't have anything to fight for. When you don't have anything to fight for, it becomes easy to lose your drive and the discipline necessary to succeed. It can even make it impossible to take the first step that starts your journey.

It's not the means, but the *Why* that drives success. Your attitude toward money is important. It's what drives your behaviors. But what creates your attitude? Your mindset.

Your mindset creates your philosophy, creates your attitude, creates your actions, creates your results, creates your life.

Without a *Why*, no one can truly help you. If you can't articulate what your why is, you are not able to put your hand up in the world and say, "Hey, I'm looking for this." If you simply tell people what you want, what you are looking for, the law of attraction dictates that those things will come to you.

The Pitcher of Opportunity

However, you have to be ready when those things come. When I reached the point in my journey where I wanted to do something different, where I wanted to follow my *Why* and leave corporate America, I was able to make that difficult decision and take the leap because I had saved 50 percent of my income. I had a buffer which allowed me to make a calculated move to get closer to where I wanted to be. I continued to do this until I reached where I am today.

In order to have the freedom to leave the broker dealer, to leave that corporate life, I had to put down the cup of scarcity in order to pick up the pitcher of opportunity—but having that financial buffer made it much easier to put that cup down.

Once you've identified what you're trying to do, the decision to put down the cup, to follow that path, becomes much easier. But it's even easier if you are financially stable and have built a reserve fund. You want to have liquidity available for new opportunities that present themselves.

My personal *Why* for my money is always getting better and more productive and powerful because I am able to take those calculated risks. I am able to make financial decisions based on my own terms, not someone else's. I'm not dictated by anything or anyone else. I can move and maneuver through all these circumstances and opportunities of my own volition. People will sometimes say to me, "You've always made really good choices in life." My response is, "Success is when preparation meets opportunity, and I've set myself up to be able to make those choices on my own terms and conditions."

Ultimately, money is not the end goal. Money is simply the fuel that helps you live your Why.

When you are financially prepared, you can take advantage of the opportunities that present themselves. You can make the moves you need to make in order to accelerate toward your destination. Because ultimately, money is not the end goal. Your *Why* is bigger than money itself. Money is simply the fuel that helps you get to that destination, to the life you want to live. Money is simply the fuel that helps you live your *Why*.

Finding Your Why: Seven Things You Must Know About Yourself

In order to truly have financial freedom it is imperative to discover your *Why*.

- What are your hopes and dreams, for you individually and together as a family?
- What are you trying to accomplish?
- Why do you work—and when you work, is it fulfilling? Is it helping you live the life you want?
- When you're not at work, what do you want to do?
- If you had the perfect day, what would your recreation look like? Is it going out and playing tennis with the kids? Is it attending a fishing tournament or going golfing with your friends?
- What does recreation mean to you?

- What moves you in life?
- What drives you forward?

These important questions will help you discover who you want to spend your time with and what your purpose will be. Then, after you find your *Why*, you must share it with the most important *Who*s in your life so they can help you achieve it.

There are seven things you must know about yourself in order to find your *Why*.

The You5™

First, there are the You5™:

1. What are your core values to live by? Are they documented and followed by all of your trusted advisors and the closest people in your inner circle? Do you have a ranking system to help you evaluate if these people fit your most important lifetime values? If they don't fit your values, what do you do about it?

   For individuals and organizations that have a set of core values, it can be important to document and communicate those values to your trusted advisors and inner circle. This can help ensure everyone is on the same page and working towards the same goals.

2. What are the three to five most important lifetime goals you want to accomplish?

   To determine your most important lifetime goals, start by asking yourself what you want to achieve in your life. What are the things that are most important to you?

What are your passions and interests? What do you want to be remembered for?

Here are some steps you can take:

- Brainstorm: Make a list of all the things you want to accomplish in your life, no matter how big or small.
- Prioritize: Review your list and prioritize your goals based on what is most important to you. You may want to categorize them into short-term, medium-term, and long-term goals.
- Refine: Take your top three to five goals and refine them to make them specific, measurable, achievable, relevant, and time-bound (SMART).
- Take Action: Once you have identified your most important goals, create an action plan to achieve them. Break them down into smaller, manageable steps, and set deadlines for each step.

Remember, your goals may change over time as your priorities shift, and that's okay. It's important to revisit your goals regularly to ensure they are still aligned with your values and aspirations.

3. What is your mission statement?

A mission statement is a concise declaration of your purpose and what you want to achieve. It should capture your values, beliefs, and what you want to contribute to the world.

To create a mission statement, you can start by asking yourself the following questions:

- What is important to me?

- What do I want to achieve in my life?
- What do I want to be known for?
- What are my values and beliefs?
- What impact do I want to have on the world?
- What problems do I want to solve?

Once you have answered these questions, you can use the following formula to craft your mission statement:

My mission is to [what you want to achieve] so that [why it matters and the impact it will have].

Make sure to keep your mission statement concise and clear. It should be something that inspires you and reflects your passion, values, and purpose. Once you have created your mission statement, you can document it and share it with the world to help you stay focused and motivated on achieving your goals.

4. What is your picture of where you want to be in the next three years? Can you close your eyes and see it?

Picturing what you want your entire lifetime to look like can be difficult to do in detail. You may be able to envision the big picture of what you want your whole life to be, but that horizon is so huge and far off it can be hard to see clearly. Instead, picture what you want your life to look like three years from now. Picture it in as much detail as you can. Maybe you've got a new house, maybe you're married and have kids, maybe you're traveling the world with your family.

If we were to sit here three years from now, what would have to happen, personally and professionally, for you to look upon our time together and say, "That was well worth it?"

Write out what this three-year picture looks like. Create a vision board. Document it in a tangible way you can share with others. Clearly visualize yourself three years from now, and we can then work backward to establish the steps to get you there.

5. What is your guarantee to the world? What is the most important thing you have to offer?

   For example, our promise at Invst is to educate, guide, and counsel people so they can reach their full financial potential. My personal guarantee is to use the tools I have to help people find financial freedom.

Two Discoveries

After the You5™, there are two Discoveries you must make about yourself:

6. What are the things you are most gifted at doing, that you can do all day and never tire of, that actually give you energy? This is what Dan Sullivan at Strategic Coach calls your Unique Ability®. Your Unique Ability® is like Under Armour: it underlies everything and equips you to reach your full potential.

   Your Unique Ability® is something you are always discovering and rediscovering about yourself. As you grow and learn more and mature and gain experience and knowledge and wisdom, your Under Armour keeps getting better.

7. What are your D.O.S.®—your dangers, opportunities, and strengths? Have you identified all the dangers that can stop you from achieving your three-year plan? Do you know what opportunities are in front of you that you should capitalize on? Have you identified your strengths that will help you get there?

   To help you identify your D.O.S.® we use the D.O.S.® process developed by Dan Sullivan.[8] We go through how you can think deeper about what those dangers, opportunities, and strengths are so you can make a decision that will put you in a better position, provide even greater opportunities, maximize your strengths, and eliminate dangers. What are your top three dangers to eliminate? What are your top three opportunities to explore? What are your top three strengths to be reinforced and maximized?

   If you can solve your dangers, capitalize on your opportunities, and maximize your strengths, you can achieve just about anything. You can truly focus on where you are today and discover yourself—and those discoveries can lead you back to all the things you need to know about yourself: your core values, your lifetime goals, your mission, your three-year picture, your guarantee to the world.

What Is Your Lifetime Perspective?

Your *Why* ultimately relates to your whole life. Having a lifetime perspective lets you intentionally plan your daily activities in relation to a much larger picture. You can use your lifetime as an inspiring goal-setting and planning tool so you can align your daily actions with your most important lifetime goals.

To help you gain this lifetime perspective and understand your *Why* for money, we use a series of tools to uncover your lifetime perspective. This process starts with a rather morbid question: if you were to die today, would your life be complete?

Gary Brackett, a good friend of mine who played for the Colts, had a very rough upbringing, including losing his mother, father, and brother in under two years. When his brother was shot and killed, Gary had to sign off on what the tombstone would read—and when they handed him the paperwork, they had accidentally put his name as the one going on the tombstone, instead of his brother's. In that moment, Gary had an immediate vision of what his life had been so far, and how much he would leave undone if he had passed away—if this was in fact his tombstone.

After this experience, Gary knew he wanted to do more with his life—and he did. He went on to win a Super Bowl with the Colts and created the Champions Academy, which helps people clarify their goals, control their habits, and become high performers across all areas of their lives.

If you were to pass away today, what would your life look like? What would others put on your tombstone today? What were the core values you lived by? What were your top lifetime achievements?

If you asked someone to write your eulogy, what do you think they would say? What would your family say about you? Would they say you were really present, or that you weren't home that much? Would they say you were true to your values? What would your best friends say about you? What would your preacher say about you? What would your personal trainer say about you?

Then, think about what you would *want* others to put on your tombstone, what you would *want* them to think and say about you, what you would *want* to have done by the time you die. "I would want my kids to think I was a good person," maybe, or, "I would want to give more to charity. I would want to be able to help people more. I would like to have spent more time with my family. I would like to have traveled more. I would like to have retired earlier. I would like to not have been so stressed about money all the time."

The Longevity Factor

Now, if you knew how much time you had left, what more would you want to do? If you could live longer than the expected age, what would you want to achieve? What would your life need to look like to have the significance you want it to have? What are the things you'd want to do? What are the characteristics you'd want to have?

Now that you know your *Why*, now that you are living a life of purpose, how much more time would you like? What would you like to accomplish in your lifetime? When would you like to accomplish it?

What would you do if you had an extra 30 years? Another 50 years? How much time would you want or need to accomplish everything you want to accomplish?

And if you did live to that age and accomplish all those things, what would your tombstone read? What would those closest to you say and think, now that you have discovered your *Why* and identified future achievements?

Once you have this lifetime perspective, you can map out the road, plan the safe and adaptable journey that will carry you to your destination, and properly manage the resources that will allow you to accelerate all the way there. It's just a matter of starting with the end in mind and working backwards.

Your Family *Why*

So far, we've been talking about you—but we know you are not the only person you care about. Financial freedom is not just for you and your future alone, but for your family and your family's future as well. Once you know yourself, once you know your *Why*, you can more successfully lead and take care of your family—and help discover your family's collective *Why*.

To do this, you can build a family constitution. Just like a country's constitution, a family constitution clearly states the mission, values, and rules of your family. What do you stand for as a family? What do you prioritize? How do you encompass everybody's individual *Why*s into a unified *Why* for the family?

To create this constitution, each family member (if they are old enough) can go through the Seven Things You Must Know About Yourself. For younger kids, help them think through what their dreams are—even though these will likely change as they grow and learn and develop new skills and passions!

Then, once you have all completed your individual Seven Things, go through them as a family. How, as a family unit, would you answer those questions?

Together, these will all be intertwined and blended together to form your family constitution. Then, you can actually send that constitution to an artist, who can design a family crest that encompasses your family's values and vision!

Your Always-Evolving *Why* For Money Recap

The goal of discovering your *Why* for money is not so you can keep it to yourself. The point is to share it with those who can help you live that *Why*, so everyone on your team can be aligned. That's why the Invst process of finding your *Why* ends with the creation of a one-page document that clearly articulates what you want, what your goals are, what your values are. This is a document you can give to your most trusted advisors, to make sure everyone is aligned with your vision and values.

But your journey to discovering your *Why* is not over once you get that document in hand. None of the things we've talked about in this chapter are static—they all evolve as you and your life and your family evolve.

Say you first created your mission statement before you had kids. When you have kids, your mission may shift. It may now center around raising your kids to be kind, responsible, successful people. Your dangers, opportunities and strengths will also shift as things change in your life, and you should regularly reevaluate the current dangers in front of you, the opportunities you want to take advantage of, and your strengths—as well as your Unique Abilities®. These will feed back into your three-year plan, your lifetime goals, and your core values—all of which will continue to evolve your *Why* as you and your family continue to evolve.

This is why the Invst4Life™ process includes a 90-day meeting cadence. Every 90 days, you revisit all the elements of your *Why*—something we will talk about more in the chapter on *Acceleration*. You are always growing and discovering more about yourself, which will make your mission statement clearer and your guarantee to the world even better, which may change your lifetime goals, and which will all ultimately help your *Why* become even more brilliant.

This is why the *Why* segment of the Freedom Wheel™ sits across from the *Acceleration* segment. Part of *Acceleration* is continually revisiting, revising, updating, discovering yourself more and leveling up. *Why* feeds directly into *Acceleration*, and *Acceleration* feeds directly back into *Why*. If you are not regularly revisiting and updating your *Why*, it will fall out of alignment. Things will get off track, your values can get tilted. When you level set and level up, you accelerate, and that's when you have abundance. To achieve abundance, your *Why* has to stay on track with you as you accelerate toward the life you want to live.

To achieve abundance, your *Why* has to stay on track with you as you accelerate toward the life you want to live.

Your *Why* is used in every other part of the Freedom Wheel™. You use it to find and align your *Who*, to lay out your *Gameboard*, to establish your *Rules*, to propel your *Execution*, and ultimately to *Accelerate* you to financial freedom.

Putting Your Money To Work

When you clearly identify your *Why* for money, it allows you to clearly identify objectives for that money. Money does not have emotions—it simply needs to know where to go. When you clearly articulate what your money is for, you can program your money to do the things it's supposed to do to get you where you want to go. At Invst, we call that *making money work for people*.

The process of discovering and articulating your *Why* paints the picture of where you are going. You don't know all the twists and turns your journey will take on the way there, but you know where you're heading. You know where you want your fuel—your money—to take you, and that means you can put your money to work for you in the most effective, efficient way possible.

Having a clear mission doesn't necessarily mean you must have all the details figured out. In fact, sometimes the best ideas are the ones that seem impossible or unrealistic at first. The important thing is to have a clear goal in mind and to be willing to experiment and iterate as you work towards that goal. Once your money knows what it's working for and once you know what *you're* working for, you can align those two things to help you live the life you want, as soon as possible.

Overall, having a clear mission can be a powerful motivator and can help accelerate your journey toward the life you want to live. But it's just one piece of the puzzle, and successful accelerators and visionaries also need to be able to adapt, collaborate, and measure their progress as they work towards their goal—all of which are made possible with the other principles of the Freedom Wheel™.

Follow this QR code to access bonus content on finding your *Why*.

4

WHO

The best way to solve a problem you don't know how to solve is to find someone who already knows how to solve it.

—Scott Jarred

You've probably heard the old aphorism: it's not what you know, but *who* you know. You've figured out your *Why*—the question now is: *Who* is going to help you get there? *Who* is going to get you across the finish line to financial freedom and the life you want to live?

If your *Why* is your destination and money is the fuel for your journey, your *Who* are the people who keep your car running—and who make sure it's running as efficiently and effectively as possible. You can have all the fuel in the world and know exactly where you are going—but if you don't have a working car, you still aren't going to get very far on your journey.

You likely already have people working on various aspects of your personal life—property casualty agent, cash flow banker, mortgage broker, stockbroker, CPA, realtor, financial planner, 401(k) expert, bookkeeper, accountant, business attorney, estate planning attorney, captive insurance attorney, life insurance agent, health insurance agent.... The list goes on.

The average person interacts with 13 financial institutions at any given time—each with their own agenda. Typically, there is no collaboration, no coordination, no communication, and no accountability. Most decisions are made in a vacuum. Advice comes from specialists in their given area of expertise, and those specialists rarely meet together to make joint decisions on your behalf. Each specialist provides advice in a silo. Without a coherent process to follow, much of their advice may not align with your vision.

Instead, you have all these microeconomic decisions being made without looking at the whole macroeconomic view of your financial world—never mind taking into consideration your values and the life you want to live. You have all these people telling you what to do and how to do it, but they don't have all the necessary data—and they're not aligned with your *Why*.

When was the last time all of your different advisors came together to help you make a unified decision? The answer is probably never. Unless you have a family office with all these advisors on payroll, you have almost certainly never had all of them together in one conversation.

That's a secret of the uber wealthy: they have so much wealth, they are able to hire their trusted advisors to work full time solely for the family. They create a family office, in which this group of trusted advisors can work together to run the family's money, abiding by and unified behind the specific rules and agenda the family office creates for them, based on their family trust or family constitution.

Here's a secret: you can create this same infrastructure the wealthiest use to manage their money. You can have the same kind of focused, aligned group of strategic advisors even if you don't have the resources to hire them on as full-time staff. You don't have to be Jeff Bezos to have an amazing team of trusted financial advisors making your money work for you.

Invst has identified and developed a process for weighing and measuring all your financial advisors to make sure they are the right fit, and to ensure they are making the right decisions for you. Then, you can operate very similarly to a family office, knowing you have a team of advisors who are going to help you reach financial freedom faster by accelerating your growth. This is your strategic Board of Directors—a team of advisors who coordinate, collaborate and communicate on your behalf.

Your Board of Directors

Your Board of Directors will include people like:

- Your CPA
- Your attorney or attorneys (an estate planning attorney, a litigator, a business attorney, etc., depending on your needs)
- Your property insurance agents (car insurance, homeowner's insurance, liability, etc.)
- Your health insurance broker
- Your employer benefits person at work
- Your disability insurance carrier

- Your life insurance carrier
- Your investment manager
- The banker who helps you with cash management
- The banker who helps you with loans (mortgages, commercial loans, etc.)
- The real estate agent who helps you find and purchase property
- Anyone across all areas of your life who assists you with your financial matters and decisions

These people all have skillsets different from yours. They understand their areas of expertise—and can use their skill and expertise to help you. But they will only be effective—and you will only be effective in finding and aligning them—if you have purpose. You have to understand your *Why*, what you are trying to do, what your destination is. Only then can you go out into the world and find the people who can help you achieve it.

Making sure your vision, purpose, and *Why* are completely clear is the first step to finding your *Who*. Then, you can use all the aspects of your *Why* to identify what people are right for which seats on your Board.

There are people in the world who won't have the same values as you. There are people who won't want to help you. There are people who won't understand what you want to do. And there are people who may have the same values, who may want to help you, who may understand you—but they don't have the ability or the availability. They don't have quite the right skillset, or they are too busy, and they would not be able to perform well for you.

There are also people who simply don't do the work. I was down in Palm Beach with a very wealthy client, and he said to me, "What I like about you is you actually work." Most of the advisors in wealthy communities like Palm Beach sit on the golf course or in the yacht clubs all day trying to build relationships. They use their relationship-building skills to make you feel good and well-liked. They get you access to all this fun stuff. But at the end of the day, are they really giving you results? Are they really aligning with you and getting you where you want to go? Do they really have your money under control? Do they really have the tools to help you reach financial freedom faster? It's all smoke and mirrors—it looks great, as long as you don't look at what's going on behind the curtain.

The Advisor Accelerator™

To help you weigh and measure all these aspects, we've created a tool called the Advisor Accelerator™. This tool is based on the wonderful People Analyzer tool created by Gino Wickman for EOS.[9] The People Analyzer is designed to help businesses find the right people. We have adapted and modified this tool into a new version that is designed to help you find the right people for your personal finances.

The Advisor Accelerator™ is a series of questions to ask each of your advisors to determine whether they are the right fit for your Board of Directors. The questions fall into four main categories:

- Do they share your values?

  In finding your *Why*, you identified your and your family's core values. Does the advisor align with these values?

A ranking system can also be helpful to evaluate whether individuals in your inner circle align with your most important lifetime values. This could involve assigning a numerical value or ranking to each value, and then evaluating whether someone's actions and behavior are consistent with those values.

If someone in your inner circle doesn't fit with your most important lifetime values, it can be important to address the situation and determine the best course of action. This could involve having a conversation with the individual to express your concerns and expectations, or it could involve making the difficult decision to distance yourself from that person if their behavior is harmful or inconsistent with your values. Ultimately, it's up to you to determine what is most important to you and how you want to live your life in accordance with your values.

- Do they understand what you are trying to do?

  When you share your *Why*, does the advisor understand what you are trying to achieve?

- Do they want to help you?

  Is the advisor inspired and motivated to help you get to your *Why*, to the life you want to live?

- Are they able and available to do the work?

  Does the advisor have the appropriate skillset to help you achieve what you want to achieve? Do they have the time to do that work to the best of their ability?

In your life, you'll have several different Boards of Directors. There's your personal Board of Directors—your life coach, your fitness trainer, your nutritionist, your therapist, your physician, your preacher or spiritual leader—people who help you get clarity on who you are and help you become an even better version of yourself. You may also have a Board of Directors for your business or professional life. For example, if you're a real estate developer, you probably have an architect and/or engineer on your Board. You may have a business coach—for example, mine is Dan Sullivan. While the Invst strategy is focused on your financial Board of Directors, this tool can be transferred to all of the trusted advisors in your life.

Your Personal CFO

Even if all your advisors are aligned, it's still a lot of people to manage. This is where the role of your Personal CFO, which we talked about in Chapter 2, comes into focus. Your Personal CFO is the connective tissue, helping you collect and organize your data, collect your thoughts, and communicate with your Board so they can make the best financial decisions to help you reach your *Why*.

Your Personal CFO keeps track of whether your Board is successfully moving you in the right direction to reach your financial freedom faster. To do this, Invst has created a Financial Life Scorecard™—something we'll discuss more in Chapter 6.

Your CFO collects all the important documents and recommendations from all your advisors and collates them in one place, so you and your Board can easily keep track of your whole financial life and how all the pieces connect. At Invst, we use the best technological tools at our disposal to do this. That's how we are able to help millions of people live the life they want! But while we do use some AI tools to help us manage all your financial information, we also believe in the human *Who*. There will always be an actual person you can talk to, who understands you and what you want, who truly knows you, your values, and your *Why*. We mix the best technology with the all-important human element.

Your Personal CFO also creates an expectation of what each advisor is accountable for. For example, your CPA is accountable for finding you the most deductions possible without crossing any legal lines, and they are accountable for being proactive about your tax planning. Your legal team is accountable for making sure you pay the least amount of estate taxes possible and making sure your money goes to who you want, where you want, when you want, under your own terms and conditions.

Your Personal CFO helps you craft three to five core responsibilities for each advisor, and then tracks whether each advisor is getting the results they are accountable for. While your Personal CFO may sometimes do this through annual meetings with your whole Board of Directors, more often they will have one-on-one meetings with each advisor, making sure the advisor's responsibilities are clear and aligned so they can do their job in the most efficient, effective way. And if someone on your Board is not fulfilling their responsibilities, if they are not achieving results, if they are not on track with keeping you on track—your Personal CFO will let them go.

Unfortunately, letting people go is sometimes a sad reality of having a high-functioning Board of Directors. When you are evaluating your advisors with the Advisor Accelerator™, if one doesn't share your core values, doesn't understand or believe in what you are trying to do, or doesn't have ability or availability, they potentially need to be replaced. They have to get it, want it, and have the capacity to do the job.

Sometimes, people will keep an advisor on because their values are aligned, but the advisor is not doing good work. We see that frequently with CPAs. For example, a small business owner will start out working with his buddy who is a CPA. That buddy did a great job when the business was a two-person shop, but when the business grows to a 50-employee firm, they simply no longer have an adequate skillset. Holding onto an advisor in this situation can negatively impact your growth and slow down your acceleration.

If you have to let an advisor go—or if you are missing a key advisor—and don't know where to look, Invst has a bench full of trusted advisors and can see who among them fits your core values and can align with your vision. Personally, I always look for people who are hungry, who want to win, who have the same drive as you. This is another role your Personal CFO fills: helping you find the right people for your Board of Directors.

Getting Aligned

Once your Board is assembled, your Personal CFO's job is to make sure every member *stays* aligned with your values, your purpose, and your *Why*. They should always be clear on your journey and your vision and are always working to help you reach financial freedom faster.

This can only happen if both your Personal CFO and your Board are clear on your *Why*, on where you are headed, on your lifetime goals. Your CPA may be doing great work over here, and your investment manager may be doing great work over there, but if they are not both aligned with one common destination, you won't get anywhere. It would be like a TV show where the costume designer is creating *Lord of the Rings* costumes, while the set designer is creating *Star Wars* sets—the two would not come together to tell a coherent story, even if both are amazing on their own.

What makes a sports team great is having a unified vision, purpose, and strategy. If everyone is playing their own game with no regard to what the rest of the team is doing, they are never going to win—even if the team is made up entirely of all-time greats.

If your advisors are not all moving in the same direction, you won't move forward. But if everybody is aligned with what you are trying to do, using their expertise to move you in the same direction, you will have maximum acceleration moving you toward a bigger future in a much faster, more effective, and more efficient way.

And, when a storm comes—whether it's a recession or a financial crisis or an unexpected medical expense—you can trust that everyone will gather together to protect you and keep you moving in the right direction. Out on the western plains, when a storm approaches, cows will spread out and try to run away from the storm, ultimately traveling with and into the storm. Bison, on the other hand, come together as a herd, squeeze in tight next to each other, and move through the storm together. Because they are operating as a unit, they make it through the storm by facing it head on, together. Your Board of Directors, properly aligned, will do the same.

When everyone is aligned, you can also think more creatively. You won't be stuck in a rut. In his book *Principles*, Ray Dalio talks about utilizing "idea meritocracy" to make smart investment decisions—taking the collective viewpoints of everyone in the room.[10] When everyone in the room is a smart, sophisticated person with a unique and well-informed perspective, they can weigh and measure everyone's input to make a better decision collectively.

Sports betting is a perfect example of this. A point spread is set a week before the game—and when the game happens, that point spread will, almost without fail, prove amazingly accurate. How? By aggregating the knowledge of all the people making wagers to land on the most likely outcome. That wouldn't be possible without the collective knowledge of all those betters.

In fact, this is where a self-contained family office arrangement can actually be restricting. By hiring, say, one lawyer full time, you are limiting what would be possible if you hired a lawyer who had an entire law firm behind him/her, or hired a CPA who had an entire firm behind him/her. Instead of having the collective IQ of an entire firm, you would just have the skillset and expertise of that one individual.

That is ultimately what a Board of Directors provides: a collective IQ that is much greater than the sum of its parts. And that is why it's so important to be able to articulate the elements of your *Why* clearly—and why you create that one-page recap of your *Why* you can share with your *Who*.

Who Leads You to Your Four Freedoms™

When your *Who*s are working as they should, it directly enables you to find your Four Freedoms™.

When you try to solve problems on your own, you are limited by your own experiences and where you currently are in your life. You're forced to spend all your time and energy trying to solve your financial life, which can be not only ineffective but very costly as well.

Don't struggle alone. Don't try to do it all yourself. That is a waste of time.

The best way to solve a problem you don't know how to solve is to find someone who already knows how to solve it. In the last chapter, we talked about finding your Under Armour, your Unique Ability®. Now, imagine you have a team of people who each have a Unique Ability® which, combined together, could help you solve all your problems. They have the skills and abilities that are outside your Unique Ability®—meaning they can work much more efficiently and effectively in those areas than you can.

Think about how long it takes for an attorney to study for and sit for the bar exam. Think about how long it takes for a CPA to get their certification. Think of the famous 10,000-hour rule put forth by Malcolm Gladwell, which attests that it takes around 10,000 hours to master any skill. You don't have enough hours in your lifetime to master every financial skill. Instead, assemble a Board of Directors who have each put 10,000 hours toward mastering their particular skill, their particular expertise. If you have 13 people on your Board of Directors, you now have 130,000 hours of expertise working for you!

Making decisions costs time and energy. When you make poor decisions, you have worse results, which makes you more stressed and uses up even more energy, which then causes you to make even poorer decisions. It's a vicious cycle of uncertainty, fear, and doubt.

In Dan Sullivan and Benjamin Hardy's book *Who Not How*, they note that Jeff Bezos, Warren Buffett, and Barack Obama all have the same philosophy when it comes to decision making: the fewer decisions you make each day, the better those decisions are.[11] Each time you make a decision, your brain expends energy and focus. Some researchers believe that making too many decisions in a row, especially without breaks, leads to progressively less thoughtful decisions. In fact, Bezos contends you should only make three high-impact decisions a day—ideally before lunch!

When you hire somebody to help you make good decisions, you regain energy. Then, you have the energy to make better decisions that will produce excellent results, thanks to your advisors' areas of expertise.

Completing tasks also costs time and energy. The less time you're using to complete tasks, the more effective you are going to be. With a Personal CFO, you don't have to micromanage every one of your advisors anymore. You know what their results are going to be, because you know they have clearly outlined responsibilities aligned with your *Why*. This team is invested in making sure you're accomplishing your goal, and they are each able to work efficiently, effectively, and independently, because they know exactly what they are all working toward. And instead of spending time in a dozen different meetings with each of your individual advisors, you can just have one meeting with your Personal CFO.

If you don't have to worry day in and day out about completing tasks and making decisions regarding your personal financial affairs, think of the capacity you'll have for other decisions in your life. You're not unnecessarily expending time and energy in those areas. You'll have more time to do the things you really care about—in other words, Freedom of Time. You'll have that time free to spend

If you don't have to worry day in and day out about completing tasks and making decisions regarding your personal financial affairs, think of the capacity you'll have for other decisions in your life.

in the way you want, with the people you want—Freedom of Relationships. You'll have time to focus on your Unique Ability®, instead of giving all this time and energy to something that is not your Unique Ability®. You can focus on your *Why*—Freedom of Purpose. Meanwhile, your *Who* are creating wealth for you so you can have Freedom of Money to enable all the other freedoms.

Go All In

If you want your *Who* to be effective so they can get you to your Four Freedoms™, you have to be fully engaged. You have to be all in. I hear so many people say, "Oh, but hiring all those people costs so much money." Yes, hiring all these advisors costs money—but it will ultimately both save you money *and* make you money. At Invst, for example, we try to find lost money and put it back to work—and often find $2 to $5 million of long-term wealth lost through inefficiency. While most plans focus on cost and taking risk, your plan should work with less risk and more efficiency. Focusing only on the initial cost is a symptom of a scarcity mindset. Seeing what that cost can gain you in the future—such as $2 to $5 million in lost wealth!—is the mindset of abundance.

A wealthy man I know—a real estate developer with billions of dollars of real estate—has legal fees that cost him multiple millions of dollars every year. "How the heck do you spend millions of dollars every year on your legal expenses?" I asked him once. "That seems crazy to me."

He looked at me and said, "You know, attorneys are really cheap partners. I hire them for their expertise, they keep me out of a lot of trouble, they help me add value—and they don't get equity in my business. I'll gladly spend millions on really good legal work because I know it will help me in what I'm trying to do." Having an attorney as a *Who* saves him a ton of money in the long term.

Even if you make the financial commitment to build your Board, it can only function if you trust them. You have to be ready to give it your all, to commit to and trust your Board of Directors and your Personal CFO.

Occasionally we encounter people who don't want to give it their all. Something internally is holding them back from releasing and trusting. Again, it's a symptom of a scarcity mindset and is often due to something they've experienced in their past. They can't fully commit or trust because they haven't overcome this issue.

I understand where they are coming from. Growing up with no money, I was always surrounded by people who were trying to rip me off or take advantage of me in some way. I always thought it was better to do it myself because I was the only one I could really trust. I considered myself very street savvy, able to figure it all out on my own.

Of course, I later realized what real street savvy people do: they have a trusted network of advisors and associates working for them. Collaborating with other people will help you transform your thinking to create an even greater *Why* for yourself and your family.

Collaboration Is Key

I've experienced this as part of Dan Sullivan's Free Zone, which gathers together successful people with different skills to create new opportunities that have never existed before. I get better because I have so many good people around me. It's why people who go to the highest-level schools typically have better opportunities—because they are surrounded by other smart, driven, passionate people.

No great progress or innovation has ever happened without some form of collaboration, without working with others to achieve a result. Taylor Swift is able to sell $1500 tickets to her concerts not just because of whatever artistic talent she has. It's because of all the incredibly skilled people she has surrounded herself with—the choreographers and managers and marketing team and audio technicians and countless others—who have enabled her to perform at such a high level. They set her up for success.

This is true of every superstar performer, from Frank Sinatra to Beyoncé. And when they have their *Who* in place to take care of the rest, the talent can just perform. They can just do what they are best at and live their *Why*, because they have trusted producers and managers and designers taking care of everything else.

Collaboration is what will help you grow and succeed—but it can only happen if you let your guard down and learn to trust other people. When your *Who* is truly aligned with your *Why*, you *know* you can trust them to always act in your best interest. You are setting the rules, you are setting the accountability, you are setting the destination. You can trust that you are all moving in the same direction.

Without a highly skilled and trusted pit crew, a racecar driver would never make it to the finish line. Assembled correctly, your *Who* will have the skills, expertise, years of knowledge, and their own list of hacks they can use to help you accelerate. Imagine how much further and faster you can go with a team like that in your corner!

When you find the right people, you can achieve top quality results at incredible speeds. Your *Who* is the ultimate hack, the ultimate shortcut—the ultimate accelerant on your journey to the life you want to live.

Follow this QR code to access bonus content on assembling your *Who*.

5

GAMEBOARD

Doing the basic skills at an elite level will make you elite.

—Scott Jarred

Imagine trying to play chess, but you don't know the rules of the game. You don't know how each piece is supposed to move. You don't know where they go on the gameboard. You don't even have a gameboard to play on. How are you supposed to win?

The answer is simple: you won't.

The same is true in the world of personal finance. You need to understand the rules of the game. You need to know how all the different pieces work. And you need a *Gameboard* to play on.

Each piece of your financial life has a different power—just as each piece on a chess board has a different power. Cash that sits in a checking account has a different power than a piece of real estate that generates cash flow, which has a different power than an investment account or a dividend-paying stock that provides income.

If you don't understand:

- the power of each piece
- how each piece moves
- how the board is laid out
- how all the pieces are organized
- how moving one piece affects the others and changes the course of the game going forward

—you'll never be able to win. You'll never be able to reach financial freedom.

Your Financial *Gameboard*™ takes all those disparate, disorganized pieces of your financial life, organizes them, and clarifies the power of each piece. A Financial *Gameboard*™ is the opposite of the financial junk drawer that constitutes most people's financial life.

Without a Financial *Gameboard*™, your financial life will likely be uncoordinated and non-integrated. Your decisions will be based on opinion and emotion and will be limited to specific needs and events rather than larger goals. Purchases will be made by convenience rather than with planning. Your information will be disorganized and inaccessible. And it will be very hard to adequately adapt to change.

That doesn't sound like a very comfortable world to live in, does it? It likely makes you feel anxious, frustrated, worried—a world that makes you stay where you are, uncertain what to do, apprehensive about moving forward on your journey.

With a Financial *Gameboard*™,

- Your financial life will be coordinated and integrated
- Your decisions can be made based on data and facts
- Your goals can extend beyond your immediate needs and into the future
- Your plans and decisions can be easily implemented because your data and information are organized and accessible.

With a Financial *Gameboard*™, you are in control. You can focus. You can have the confidence to accelerate forward on your journey to financial freedom so you can live the life you want.

The Four Dimensions

The Financial *Gameboard*™ is indebted to a series of financial models created by great financial minds. Robert Kiyosaki, author of *Rich Dad, Poor Dad*, built a system called the Cashflow Quadrant. Bob Castiglione created the Lifetime Economic Acceleration Process, or LEAP, which incorporated protection, savings and growth in order to weigh and measure financial decisions. However, LEAP did not really include net worth in its calculations. Bob Ball, who also worked on the LEAP system, built a product called the Living Balance Sheet, which uses a financial house structure to weigh and measure decisions.

The Financial *Gameboard*™ is an evolution of this financial house.

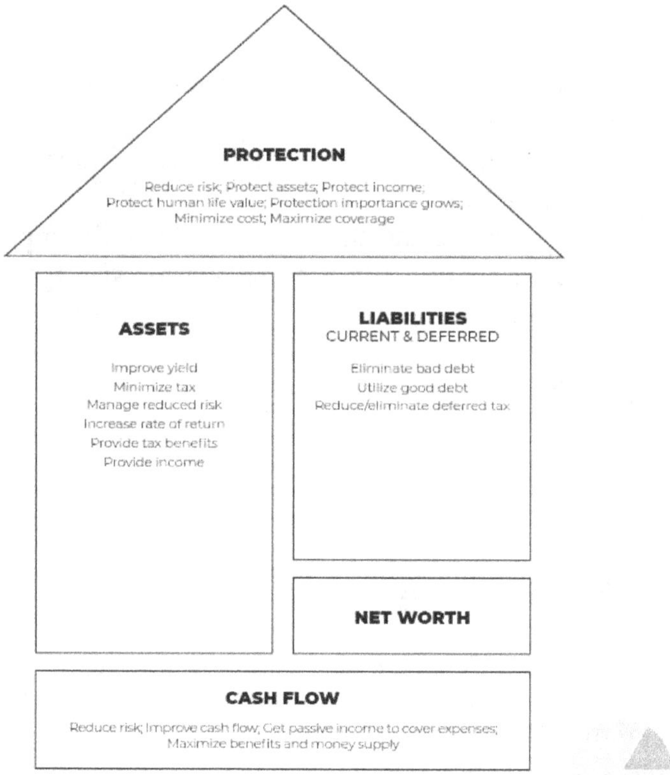

©2022 INVST. All rights reserved

Your game board needs to cover four critical dimensions:

- Cash Flow
- Assets
- Liability
- Protection

Cash Flow

To build a stable house, you first need a solid foundation. For your financial life, that foundation is your cash flow. Understanding how money flows in and out of your house is critical. How is your cash flow organized? Where does the money go first? When you understand this, you can see where you are leaking money, where there is lost opportunity cost. Is money leaking to pay off debts? Are you paying too much in taxes? Are your insurance costs not lining up? Are you putting money toward lifestyle first, rather than paying yourself first? In the coming chapters, we'll get into the right way to manage and prioritize your cash flow.

Inside your house are your assets and your liabilities.

Assets

Your assets include your:

- Savings
- Investments
- Cash value life insurance
- Retirement accounts
- Personal property
- Real estate
- Business assets
- Illiquid assets
- Liquid assets

Liabilities

Liabilities include both good debt and bad debt, short-term debt and long-term debt. The goal is to eliminate your bad debt first and understand how to utilize your good debt, which has tax deductions, low interest rates, and is attached to appreciating assets. Bad debt, such as credit card debt, has high interest rates, no tax benefits, and is attached to depreciating assets.

Liabilities can also be your hidden tax liability—for example, the tax liability in your traditional retirement accounts and in capital gain tax. It is important to know your liabilities in making financial decisions.

Your assets minus your liabilities equals your Net Worth, which is also contained within your house.

Protection

You would never move your family and all your belongings into a house unless you were sure the roof wouldn't leak or cave in. Just the same, you want to protect your financial house. You want a strong roof to shield everything inside from anything that might cause damage. You want to protect your assets and your income. You want to protect yourself legally. And you want to protect your legacy. Each of these protections has different powers—and for each, you need to consider the "What Ifs."

"What Ifs" are all too often neglected. You need to protect yourself from the unforeseen. Without proper protection, your whole house, your whole *Gameboard*, can be knocked off course. If your house is damaged in a flood and you don't have flood coverage, your house may be worth less, but you may still owe the same amount on your mortgage. That knocks your net worth out of balance.

Of course, there's no way to know whether your house will ever be damaged in a flood—but you still need to have that liability protection in place. Protection gives you permission to live your life—and enjoy your money—free of worry. Having perfect protection means no longer having to worry about being financially exposed to the catastrophic happenings of life.

Making Moves on the *Gameboard*

Your Financial *Gameboard*™ lays out and organizes those 20 pieces within your financial house so you can easily weigh and measure each of them when you make financial decisions. It helps you see each of the four dimensions clearly and understand how they interact, so you know how a decision in one dimension will affect the others.

How do you:

- Decide between Option A and Option B and clearly see the future impact of that decision?
- Decide between a traditional IRA, a Roth IRA, or both?
- Spend all your money and still leave it to the next generation?
- Decide between starting a 401(k) or saving for your first home?
- Decide between putting money in a checking account for a cash reserve or an investment account?
- Decide between buying a car with cash, leasing it, or financing it?
- Velocitize your money to do multiple things like earn interest, defer taxes, protect yourself from creditors, death, and disability, and use the same dollar to buy cash flow real estate?

Most people make these decisions in a vacuum, without measuring the effects on Protection, Assets, Liability, and Cash Flow. You can't map out all the benefits and money supply without a Financial *Gameboard*™. Having a Financial *Gameboard*™ to weigh and measure decisions is crucial to your financial success. If you—or any one of your advisors—are making a financial decision without putting it into a financial model to weigh and measure it, then it is likely to be the wrong decision. It hasn't been battle-tested across all four dimensions.

Four Dimensional Decisions

With your *Gameboard*, instead of decisions being messy and complex, you can see the entire picture clearly and simply. You can see the macroeconomic impact of your decision from a high level, which allows you to weigh and measure all the critical domains and see all the intricacies of how that decision affects each piece on the board. When you can put every piece in the right spot, you are able to weigh and measure which moves and options are best for you and make smart, well-informed, evidence-based decisions.

Say you are buying a car. Do you lease it, pay cash for it, or finance it? If you pay cash for it, you lose control of money that could otherwise be used for future cash flow. If you get a loan for it, that could give you bad debt. If you lease it, then you're only using part of the car, and you can deduct it. With a model, you can evaluate all three of these options. Once you know what you are going to do, you can follow that course of action and set those rules for how you buy a car.

You can plug any decision into the *Gameboard* and make an informed decision instead of an emotional decision. For example, one big financial decision most people make, often more than once over the course of their life, is buying a house—whether it's a primary home or a second or vacation home. A house is very multidimensional: the house itself is an asset, the mortgage is a liability, homeowner's insurance and liability coverage are for protection.

You can plug any decision into the *Gameboard* and make an informed decision instead of an emotional decision.

Within this one big decision, there are dozens of smaller decisions to be made across all four dimensions, many pieces on the gameboard that need to be moved, and many other pieces that will be affected by those moves. For example:

- If you are getting a mortgage, what type of mortgage do you get?
- Do you know the tax benefits of the different types of mortgages?
- How do you structure ownership?
- Does your estate plan attorney know how to best title the property so it's outside the wealth transfer system to avoid paying estate taxes?
- Do you have protection if someone slips and falls in your house?
- Do you have protection if there is a lawsuit or a fire?
- How much money do you put down?
- How do you put money down with no additional out-of-pocket costs?
- What's the most effective way to do this without impacting your wealth?

Remember, lost opportunity cost means every dollar you put down loses six times its value in 30 years because you are missing out on the compounding interest on those dollars. How do you understand, weigh, and measure that lost opportunity cost? How do you recapture that money?

Your *Gameboard* helps you weigh and measure every one of these decisions. As you weigh what to do, the *Gameboard* helps you see what the dangers of that decision might be, what opportunities it might present, what strengths it might maximize. Once you identify and understand those, you can think more clearly about what move you want to make.

Consider All the Pieces

The fact is, most families have never truly considered many—if not most—of those 20 things listed in the financial house. Some they may never have considered at all. They may not have considered:

- The amount of liability coverage they have
- What benefits at work they're not maximizing
- Different ways to set up legal agreements for how they own various assets
- Proper life insurance protection
- Having enough liquidity saved up for an emergency fund
- Having enough savings they can access outside of retirement
- Losing tax deductions because they aren't aware of those deductions
- Whether they have the right kind of mortgage for their current situation
- How they may be burdened by bad debt and not utilizing good debt
- Whether they are paying for college effectively

- How to protect their full economic value from every angle—property and casualty, disability, health, life, legal
- What cash they are sitting on that is eroding with inflation because it is not being put to work
- Whether they are generating much—if any—passive income

Most people don't know what their balance sheet is, or what their net worth statement is, let alone have a profit and loss statement of their cash flow, like a business would.

Most people who have gone through the process of assembling their financial *Gameboard* will find that, of the 20 things they evaluate, they have 20 areas that can be improved. Add up all those little wins, and you will likely create $2 to $5 million in additional wealth. Doing the little things effectively creates a sum total that will help you win over the long haul. Doing the basic skills at an elite level will make you elite.

If you have a financial junk drawer, you can't see all the places where things are missing or can be improved. You may feel the nagging thought in the back of your mind that something is missing, but you can't see where it is. When you have everything laid out clearly on the *Gameboard*, you can see exactly where those missing pieces are, which pieces can be improved—and which pieces can be adjusted to keep you from losing a substantial amount of wealth later.

Four-Dimensional Protection

Here is an example of how four-dimensional protection works: We worked with a large family office in the process of building a business that was going to be worth a great deal of money. Using a Financial *Gameboard*™, we were able to put the business on the family balance sheet and project out into the future how big this business would be.

Our model showed there would be a tremendous amount of estate taxes and loss of wealth if they owned the business the way they had planned. Even though the asset would be growing immensely, they would have a massive deferred tax liability that would come due way into the future. Their net worth would be eroded by taxes, which would then impact their cash flow. They would have to come up with cash flow by selling a hard illiquid asset such as real estate or a business, potentially at the wrong time, to pay for that liability.

We protected the family by organizing and structuring the ownership of the business in their multi-generational dynasty trust to allow the value to grow outside of the tax system. We also doubled the family's net worth by insuring all the family members for their economic value, which will allow them to enjoy all their wealth if they wish or pass it on to the next generation. This not only eliminated the tax exposure—it also allows the family to have more control of their money, which enables them to spend and enjoy their money now and in the future, all while being protected from tax exposure.

Their Financial *Gameboard*™ clearly showed all four critical domains and how we could structure the business across all four dimensions. We never would have put all the pieces in the right place if we didn't have a *Gameboard* where we could see how it would all play out. Without a *Gameboard*, we would never have been able to see the potential loss of wealth. We would never have been able to foresee those future issues without putting their whole financial life on one simple *Gameboard*, as opposed to the hundreds of complex pages you usually get from a financial planner.

Once we had this Financial *Gameboard*™, we took it to the trust attorney, to the life insurance company, to business brokers and salespeople, so everyone could get on the same page. Now, we had a collection of *Who*s all moving in the right direction to solve this and any issue for the client. For every decision, the family can reference this financial *Gameboard*. Now, they and their *Who*s can maintain, update, and keep that model intact going forward.

Your Key Player

One decision could cost you millions of dollars of wealth in the future—but you would never know unless you see how that decision plays out on your *Gameboard*. This is why all companies have CFOs—strategic thinkers who can see the big financial picture and how each financial decision affects the whole gameboard. And that's why all individuals and families should have the Personal CFO we've discussed in previous chapters.

Even if you have the tools and the *Gameboard*, having someone with years of experience who knows how to play the game, plus the collective financial IQ of everything they've learned from helping thousands of clients, is invaluable.

Your *Who*s have all their expertise to offer as well, of course. They all have separate brains, but they are working collectively to make decisions with one mind to move you forward. If you have your data and *Gameboard* organized, it will help them make better decisions so they can do a better job for you.

Know Your *Who*'s Agenda

However, your *Who*s likely all have their own agendas as well, which will influence their opinions on all the factors of your decision. The realtor wants to make the biggest commission, so they want to sell you the biggest house possible. The mortgage broker wants to sell you the highest rate spread for the biggest mortgage you can possibly get. The bank wants you to do a term loan that will make you pay the most for the mortgage over a short period of time. The property and casualty company doesn't want to put the house on their profile risk, they want to try and transfer it to you. Everybody has an agenda for that one decision, and usually, nobody is *fully* aligned with you, because they are beholden to their own priorities as well. They're not fully sitting on the same side of the table as you—they can only see the decision from their point of view.

Now, for the first time, you can have a Personal CFO who is a true fiduciary, who sits with you and helps you see all the facets of the decision and how they play out on the Financial *Gameboard*™. Together, you can weigh and measure all the different options, see how they affect your whole financial life, and make sure you're making the right decision. Your Personal CFO's job is to educate, guide, and counsel you in those decisions.

Your Personal CFO manages the whole ecosystem. As the CEO of the household, you say, "I want to do this. I want to move that piece." The Personal CFO then looks at your *Gameboard* and says, "Okay, if you want to move that piece, here are all the other combinations from that one decision that could affect you in getting across the finish line." Once the decision is made, it becomes an item for execution and moves over to whoever on your Board of Directors is accountable for that execution item. Now, each *Who* will be held accountable to being 100 percent aligned with your *Why*, because you and your Personal CFO have played the decision out across your *Gameboard* to ensure it is the best decision for *you*.

Playing Into the Future

As you make one decision, one move on the *Gameboard*, you are not just making that one move in the present. You are really moving five steps ahead because you are seeing how this one decision plays out across all four dimensions before it happens. You can see what will happen if you let the strategy play itself out. A *Gameboard* allows you to project where you will be three years from now, five years from now, ten years from now, if everything stays intact. You can see whether those projections align with your three-year picture, with your ten-year goals.

And when something doesn't go to plan, when your journey gets unexpectedly sidetracked by an obstacle or unforeseen event, you can see exactly what is happening, and you have rules that will tell you exactly how to pivot to get yourself back on track. If something like a flood does happen, and it moves a piece on your *Gameboard*, you can immediately see how all the other pieces of your *Gameboard* are affected, and how to move them to counter the move the flood made. You're always three steps ahead of whatever catastrophe happens—or whatever unexpected good thing happens!

Having a model allows you to do this because you've already evaluated the What If scenarios of all the different things that could stop you in your tracks. You've already accounted for eroding factors like taxes, inflation, planned obsolescence, technological change, lawsuits, death, and disability. You have all of those What Ifs covered by having the optimal protection right now, so you can make adjustments should anything happen.

Expect the Unexpected

You can even take advantage of unexpected circumstances. In 2008 and 2009, when everyone was panicking about their investments, our investment strategies were able to adapt because they are based on rules that allow people to take advantage of the uncertainties in the economy. Our strategies actually made a lot of money for people! The same thing happened during Covid. If you have rules to follow—which we'll talk about more in Chapter 6—you don't panic. You aren't shaken by uncertainty, your finances aren't in chaos, because you have a Financial *Gameboard*™ and rules to keep you on track, no matter what happens. Not only will your journey be smooth—you may even come out the other side better! Our clients made huge gains in 2008 and 2009 and during Covid, and they're going to make even bigger gains coming out of 2022 and 2023.

These events happened in the macroeconomy of the world and the country, but unexpected events also happen in the personal economy of your family. If you truly know your present position today, you can forecast what it will look like in the future. You can't forecast what exactly will happen if there's a hailstorm. You don't know for certain your roof won't cave in or leak. But you do know you are protected for your full value by insurance to get back what you may lose. You know your foundation will stay strong and secure. You know your assets, liabilities, and net worth will be protected.

Of course, lifetime events can also be positive, not just negative! It could be a grandchild being born, or an unexpected job opportunity, or a chance to take an amazing trip with your family. You can say, "Okay, I want to take this job. How would that move affect all the other pieces on my *Gameboard*? How would it affect my protection? What did I have at my old company, and what will I have at the new company? How does it affect my assets? Do I have to spend any of my assets to create new liabilities in the new place I live?"

Build a Financial Model That Can Adapt to Change

This is the difference between a plan and a model. A plan is static and assumes things will happen in a linear way. A model is made up of moving pieces that can all adjust to whatever comes down the road. A plan looks at a future set of assumptions. A model looks at your present position. Today, are you protected in the right way across all areas of your financial life? Say your income goes up. Has your protection adjusted to cover that increased income? Have you adjusted your savings percentage rates? Have you adjusted your life insurance?

A model is all about positioning, while planning is about trying to predict the future with certainty. A model is a living, breathing thing, adjusting and optimizing as you move through life, putting you in the best position possible to weather—or take advantage of—whatever comes your way.

To put it another way, a financial plan is like printed out MapQuest directions. There's a reason no one uses those anymore! They can't automatically update and adjust based on road closures or detours or wanting to pull off the highway to go out to a scenic outlook to see the view. A financial model, a *Gameboard*, is like a live car computer with a GPS combined with the sensors that come with today's most high-tech electric cars. It has your path mapped out, and it also has the current traffic conditions. It can tell you when a pedestrian is crossing in front of or behind your car. If you start drifting over the line, it beeps to let you know you need to get back on track. It has automatic traction control. It knows where the speed traps are, where the road closures are.

A model looks into the future and says, "Here are the obstacles that might be in your way, and here is how you maneuver to get through those. And here are the good things that might happen, and how to best take advantage of those."

This is why your *Gameboard* is the third component of the peace and harmony half of the Freedom Wheel™. You can go through life with peace and harmony knowing your information is ready on your *Gameboard* for any What Ifs that might come your way, knowing your *Who*s are around you able to do the best job possible because they have your *Gameboard*, and knowing that it is all aligned around your *Why* to take you to the next level.

Your CFO will lay out the *Gameboard* and make sure every piece on the board has been vetted, and every player—your *Who*—has the rules and evidence they need to follow. Your CFO will help leverage those pieces to help you win the game as fast as possible—and make sure you are playing the game you want to play.

With a *Gameboard*, you can feel completely secure and confident because all the checks and balances are in place. With that infrastructure built, you can confidently accelerate your journey to the life you want to live!

Follow this QR code to access bonus content on setting up and using your *Gameboard.*

6

RULES

Ultimately, the only one who can set your rules is you.

—Scott Jarred

You've got your *Who* in place and your *Gameboard* assembled—now it's time to set the *Rules* of the game.

If you don't have rules for your money, someone else will. As we talked about in Chapter 1, financial institutions have their rules. If you don't have your own set of rules to play by, you'll end up playing by their rules, and there's no way to win if you're playing by their rules. Money always finds a home, and it's usually with the person (or institution) that has the best rules.

Rules are a crucial tool sophisticated investors use to stick to their game plan. *Rules* will keep you on the road when things get tough, and they keep you out of the valley of bad decisions.

All the great wealth builders have not only principles—they also have specific rules for their money. Warren Buffett, for instance, believes in investing in value and holding for the long term. He wants to build wealth in the most tax-efficient way possible and leave multi-generational wealth to impact global humanity. He's never paid a dividend. He created rules for his money that make all this happen. Ray Dalio wants his money to last for the next generation. He created the All-Weather portfolio, which is a set of rules that will dictate how his family trust money is managed when he's not there. Many other successful people have adopted this set of rules.

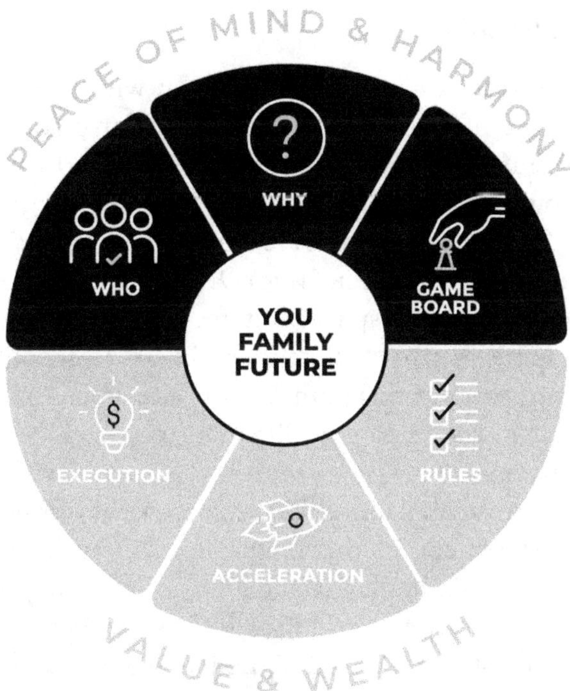

To be successful with your money, it's vital to establish rules based on evidence-backed processes that will stand the test of time. Each piece on your Financial *Gameboard*™—each of those 20 items in your financial house, across all four dimensions—will have rules. Like in chess, each piece has its individual power and limitations—a King or a Queen or a Rook can only do certain things. But unlike chess, where the rules are already set, the Invst4Life™ process is designed to work with you to create your own unique set of rules for your *Gameboard* and your game, specific to you. We use what we know to be true about the game to create a playing style that works best for you and your family.

Setting Your *Rules*

Your *Rules* should align with your *Why*, with your core values, with the life you want to live. Your Personal CFO can help you craft your *Rules* based on evidence and what works for you, but ultimately, the only one who can set those rules is you. You shouldn't compare yourself to others because each person has a different InvstDNA™ and your rules are designed and tailored specifically for *you*, not someone else. The comparison game didn't work in grade school, and it surely won't work at this point in your life. Focus on creating rules that are coded to your lifestyle, to your DNA, to you and your family.

Most financial plans will have some kind of rules to follow. Unfortunately, in the financial industry, "rules" often means a long inscrutable list someone rattles off to you, which you then promptly forget. With Invst4Life™, the rules are different. Invst4Life™ is designed to take you through a discovery process to develop your own rules. That way, you not only know what the rules are—you will remember them, because you created them yourself, so you truly understand them, have ownership over them, and believe in them.

At the end of the day, your *Rules* are built by you and for you, for your family, and for your future—and the only way they work is with your active engagement to put them into place. You should be the CEO and owner of the financial institution that is your household. Your Personal CFO helps you weigh and measure each decision you want to make and helps guide and counsel you through these processes.

Once those *Rules* are set, your entire team is held to those rules. Your Personal CFO, your entire Board of Directors, all of your *Who*s will follow these same *Rules*. Your entire team will be playing the same game—and playing for you to win.

Your InvstDNA™

Phase one of managing your money is understanding your InvstDNA™. Your InvstDNA™ ties back to your *Why* for money. Why do you invest? It's not to beat the market, become the richest person in town, or prove how smart you are. You invest for specific wants—retirement, college, buying a house and so on—but most importantly, you invest to be able to live the life you want.

That's why Invst4Life™ takes you on a journey to discover what evidence-backed investment rules and strategies work for you, to discover your InvstDNA™. We create a contract for you with yourself—an investment policy statement—that lays out your InvstDNA™. It reminds you of the decisions you've made, why you made those decisions, and what the long-term impact of those decisions will be.

There are three key components to determining your InvstDNA™: your InvstIQ™, your Invst XQ™, and your InvstEQ™. InvstIQ™ is your basic understanding of investments, how they work, and how they fit into your wants, needs, and goals. Your InvstXQ™ is your experience quotient. Your InvstEQ™ is your emotional behavior around investing.

To do this, we have a series of questions we ask to help get clear on how you are wired and your understanding of how your investments work—your InvstIQ™. Most people have very little idea of the basics of how the markets work. You don't need to be an expert, but you want to have a baseline understanding and you definitely don't want to invest in something you don't understand.

Your InvstXQ™ can be harder to calculate, but it is equally important. By recognizing where your experience lies, you can see how that experience impacts how you make decisions.

Your InvstEQ™ is more about your financial behavior and emotions around money:

- What do you fear?
- What are you trying to avoid?
- What biases do you carry? For example, there could be something from your childhood that impacts your financial decisions today.
- What are the hot buttons that have triggered your actions in the past and today?
- What strategies are off the table?
- What strategy would you be interested in learning more about?

Behavioral finance is a huge component of reaching financial freedom. One of the biggest reasons why people are not successful with their investment strategies is because they can't handle their emotional side. That's why both your

Invst IQ and EQ are essential in developing your InvstDNA™. You want to recognize both your intellectual and emotional understanding and behaviors around finance.

The best investment strategy for you is the one you can stick with long-term. If you have a strategy you can't stick with, or you want to tinker and shift strategies often (usually based on market fluctuations), then it's the wrong strategy. Once you have discovered your InvstDNA™, it is important to find a financial model and strategy that fits your DNA. In the Invst4Life™ process, there are 50 plus different evidence-based strategies to choose from that will fit any given person's InvstDNA™.

The best investment strategy for you is the one you can stick with long-term.

Risk and Reward

Matching your InvstDNA™ with the right strategy has a lot to do with your risk tolerance—how much risk you are willing to take for a given result. When making an investment decision, the first thing you need to consider is how much risk you want to take on. The second thing you need to consider is the return on that investment.

Most people think of return first, then risk. This is what led so many people into investing in things like crypto based on returns their friends had gotten or that they read about online. They didn't consider that they could lose 80 percent—or even 100 percent—of their money overnight!

If you have a 20-foot ladder, some people will want to immediately climb all the way to the top because they enjoy every second of everything that goes on up there. They aren't worried about the fall—that risk is not on their mind. But when thinking about investments and risk, you have to think about how long it will take you to recover. If you are 25 and you fall off a 20-foot ladder, chances are you'll bounce back. It will hurt for a couple weeks, maybe a couple months, but then you'll be back in the game. But as you get older, if you fall off a 20-foot ladder, it will take you out of capacity for a couple years, if not longer—if not permanently. And if you're 65 and it takes you five years or more to recover, you have less time ahead of you to return to the life you want to live.

When you put a financial strategy in place, it's important to think about the risk in how far up the ladder you are going in the first place, and what could happen once you're up there. Then, you design a strategy around that risk.

Some people don't want to climb the ladder at all. They say, "I don't want any risk of loss." In that case, you need to determine what strategies you can put your money into which are uncorrelated to the market. Assets that are completely uncorrelated with the market have no risk of loss—but you may give up returns in exchange for that lack of risk. So, you must set your plan up properly to be more tax efficient, to be even more nimble and effective.

But at some point, if you really want your money to work for you and beat inflation, you may need to take on some risk. It's imperative to limit that risk and volatility as much as possible, but if you have no risk, you're going to sacrifice some upside. And in fact, not investing is a risk as well, because of eroding factors. A dollar today is worth less than a dollar in 20 years. If your money isn't growing, it is eroding. If your money isn't working for you, as hard as it can, you are going to lose money over time just by the erosion of inflation.

Generally speaking, when you are putting together an investment strategy, you want the least amount of risk for the best result. Financial scholars and Invst4Life™ have identified and ranked all the evidence-based strategies, starting with the ones that have the least amount of risk for the best result, down to the ones that have the worst result for the most risk. You want to keep from chasing returns and put yourself in a position where you can control your destiny by having downside protection with a smooth ride—while still getting to the top of that 20-foot ladder.

Rules and Evidence

Rules and evidence are keys to that smooth ride. When you make financial decisions without rules and evidence, you are putting the ladder up without knowing how stable the ground is or how sturdy the building you're leaning the ladder against is. That's where you can get in a lot of trouble—portfolios full of investments with no rules and evidence behind them.

Most people who don't have evidence-based rules and strategies end up market timing, stock picking, trying to predict the future. We know for a fact that doesn't work over long periods of time. You've worked hard for your money. It should be managed in a way that allows a high likelihood of success over the long term.

What Does Not Work, and What Does

Here's the short list of what doesn't work:

- Market timing—guessing when to get in and out.
- Stock picking—trying to pick the next big winner.
- Performance chasing—investing in what did well in the past.
- Track-record investing—using past performance as your sole guide.

When it comes to investing, here's what works:

- Consistently and systematically invest in an evidence-based strategy that you can stick with.
- Reduce volatility. Consistent returns, even if lower, will increase your dollar growth over the long term and make for a smoother investment ride.
- Poor investor behavior is one of the surest ways to fail. Having a disciplined, rules-based approach is the best way to overcome this.
- Costs matter. Reducing the cost of investing with tax-efficient and low expense ratio strategies is key.
- Minimize downside risk. Every smart investor looks at the downside first, not the upside. Markets aren't always priced efficiently, and investors can act irrationally. This is why momentum exists, and why it's one of the best ways to capture potential from these market realities.
- Trend following is the most consistent form of active investing proven to work.
- Momentum is a persistent market anomaly that has stood the test of time, even when other factors haven't.
- Simplify the investing experience. You should fully understand how and why you're invested a certain way. This is part of crafting your personal investing philosophy that you can adhere to for the long term.

Invst4Life™'s strategies are designed based on these beliefs. They combine market realities (evidence) with academic theory (such as MPT), filling in the gaps to create a better investing experience for you. Investing is no longer about a goal, target, or magic number. It's about maximizing your financial potential with good habits, aligning your behaviors with your most important values, and controlling the factors that can limit your success to the best of your ability. You can never completely eliminate drawdowns, risk, or volatility without using insurance or some other feature. But you can apply proven principles that limit your exposure and capture potential.

If you don't put your money to work for you, you will be working for money for the rest of your life.

Your InvstDNA™ is absolutely crucial to your success because it's about how you put your money to work—and if you don't put your money to work for you, you will be working for money for the rest of your life.

The *Rules* of the *Gameboard*

People often believe the only way to get wealthy—or, at least, the only way to get wealthy quickly—is by taking big risks, especially investment risks. But your investments are just one set of pieces on your *Gameboard*—and your InvstDNA™ is just one set of *Rules*.

For example, I didn't achieve my wealth by taking investment risks. In fact, I was quite conservative. I spent ten years saving, building cash reserves, putting money into protection. I built a moat around myself as fast as I could. Then, when opportunities popped up, I could take advantage of them. I used the velocity of money to get one dollar to do multiple things to create wealth. I put my money in uncorrelated assets. I paid myself first by saving 70 percent of my income. I protected myself first. I did the opposite of what the mainstream financial institutions say to do!

My *Rules* were to protect myself for my full human life value, build up a year of core liquidity, then use velocity of money concepts to take advantage of opportunities when they presented themselves. Once I had built that up, I was able to take calculated risks knowing I was fully protected. When I won on those calculated gambles, I took my chips off the table, protected them, and played with the house's money— similar to how you beat the house in Vegas, except I made the rules. I started building my investment portfolios off the new-found money. As my investments grew, it allowed me to make another investment, then another one. I would get money back from those investments and be able to take those calculated risks again. Eventually, just the passive income from those investments was enough to give me all the cash flow I needed. That passive income replaced my income, which gave me greater power and ability to continue to build.

My whole journey was based on the fundamental foundation of paying myself first to build enough liquidity, fully protecting myself, and knowing where every dollar was going—because if I didn't, someone else would capture that money. Now, I am in control of my finances, rather than somebody else. And now, these kinds of *Rules* Invst helps you establish.

Just as you need rules for your investments, you need rules for your taxes, rules for your protection, rules for your assets, rules for your liabilities, rules for your cash flow. For example, you need to know:

- How much you want to save
- How much core liquidity you should have
- When you want to become work optional

- How much automobile insurance and liability coverage you should have to protect your human life value
- What the rules are for your estate plan, will and trust to protect and carry on your legacy
- Whether you want to incorporate philanthropy into your rules

And more. Your Personal CFO will work with you to build a unique set of *Rules* that fit you, your family, and your future.

In general, to reach your full financial potential, there are three things you must do, three simple rules you must follow:

- Organize yourself
- Pay yourself first
- Protect yourself fully and forever

Organize Yourself

Step one of organizing yourself has already been covered—your *Gameboard*. But within your *Gameboard*, across the four dimensions, there are further organizational rules you can set.

Perhaps most importantly, your cash flow order of importance is a rule you would implement. How money comes into your housc and how it leaves is important. The typical structure allows for leaks, which hinders your ability to take care of yourself, your family, and your future. As you discover how money comes in and out of your house, you'll often find the order in which you are paying things is the root of the problem.

Most people spend on lifestyle first (buying the big house or fancy car), then they pay their debt (as many financial experts recommend), then they pay their taxes, then they pay their protection, and they put what's left over—which by that point is usually not very much—into savings. The problem is compounded by the fact that each of those buckets—lifestyle, debt, taxes, and protection—are usually leaking money. The money leaking out of those buckets is the lost opportunity cost we're looking for—and because that money is leaking, people aren't saving as much as they should. They become just like the majority of Americans who are only saving three to four percent.

When you do things in this order, you lose control of your money. By the time you get to the point where you are actually starting to build wealth, you've lost out on the most crucial years of your compound interest curve. Warren Buffet believes, and I agree, that compound interest is the greatest miracle ever. If you look at a compound interest curve over a 30-year period, 50 to 75 percent of growth is on that last five to seven years of the curve.

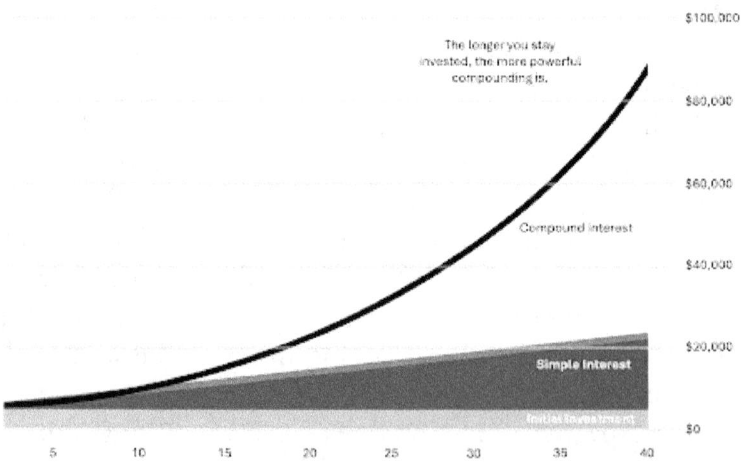

You'll see curves go from $1 million to $2 million, and that entire second million of wealth is built in those last few years. But if you haven't built up those first years, you won't get that curve in the final years.

We want to make sure you're doing things in the right order, prioritizing things in the right way. Ideally, you should save and invest—i.e. pay yourself—protect yourself, pay your taxes and debt, and then use what's left over for lifestyle.

Pay Yourself First

We believe you are your number one asset. You, your family, and your future should always come first—not last. That is why we believe you should pay yourself first.

Usually, you are the last person you take care of when you make money. The first person you pay is usually the IRS because those tax withholdings come out of your paycheck. Then you usually pay all your bills. Then you spend money on your lifestyle. And then you pay yourself.

Paying yourself first means paying your future self—setting money aside for your future self, allowing it to grow, and protecting it. The average savings rate in America is under three percent. The fact is, on average you need to save at least 15 percent, to account for five factors:

- Three percent for delayed expenditures in the in the future, such as retirement
- Three percent for inflation—everything is going up in cost
- Three percent for planned obsolescence—everything is designed to break down eventually
- Three percent for technological change—as technology advances, you'll need to upgrade your devices

- Three percent for increased standards of living—as you get older, you want nicer things (or at least your spouse might want nicer things!)

People think about setting money aside to replace their income, but not to combat these eroding factors. If you pay yourself 15 percent first, you know you have money set aside to insulate yourself from these factors. Over the next 20 to 30 years, you will have enough money to replace your current income. If you just pay yourself first, even if you blow the rest of your money, you'll be in a better spot.

Once you've paid yourself, your *Rules* take over in setting where that money goes. Ideally, you want a year of liquidity available, so if you lose your job or are unable to work, you have a full year of buffer. At the minimum, you want to have three to six months of liquidity set aside—money you can access quickly.

When you set these *Rules*, your money is programmed to do what it needs to do. Every time you get a dollar, your money is programmed to send the amount you set to savings, to pay yourself. Your money knows how much needs to go into your war chest of liquidity, so you don't have to think about it. You know you have access to the money you need when an opportunity or a danger arises. You never have to worry about not having access to cash when you need it.

Being a world-class saver (saving 15 to 20 percent) is the biggest predictor of building long-term wealth—much more important even than your investment returns. Recapturing lost money can help boost your savings amount. Money leaking from your account for inefficient insurance costs, unused subscriptions, inappropriate deductibles, high interest rate debt, and more could be robbing you of future wealth. Recapturing these lost dollars increases your velocity of money to build future wealth.

Protect Yourself Full and Forever

Very rarely do financial planners talk about protection—the least sexy but most vital subject. Protection is the most important thing to get right. If you don't, it can stop you in your tracks. And if you do get it right, it can create the most spendable, enjoyable wealth for you in the future.

You want to make sure to protect all of your assets and remain outside the wealth transfer system, minimizing or eliminating the negative impacts of estate taxes. You want to have a clearly articulated plan for what will happen when you pass away. And when you pass away, you should be able to replace every dollar you've ever made to pass on to the next generation—so that you can enjoy all of your money while you are alive. If you can do that without any additional out-of-pocket costs, you have a win-win scenario.

As you build maximum protection, you should also plan for the short-term opportunities or tragedies that could arise. That's why you build that war chest of cash—but protection needs to go beyond that moat. You have to protect yourself from the things you don't know will happen. If you were disabled or hit with a lawsuit and were unable to pay yourself first, then you would have very little chance of reaching your full financial potential. You can't control everything that happens, but you can control whether you are protected for your full value, which gives you the ability to be financially secure through whatever happens.

Protect Your Most Important Asset—You

You are your most important asset. Your ability to produce cash flow is what makes everything possible.

If you have a goose that lays golden eggs, what's more important to protect—the golden eggs, or the goose that lays them? What do you insure, the eggs or the goose? In the world today, everybody insures the eggs—your house, your cars, your belongings. But those eggs don't exist without the goose that produces them. You are your most valuable asset—but we often don't insure ourselves.

If you have a goose that lays golden eggs, what's more important to protect—the golden eggs, or the goose that lays them?

And if you are the goose that lays the golden eggs, those eggs are not just for your life—they are for your family's life as well. Replacing your income is necessary to protect both you and your loved ones. If you are sick or disabled and not able to continue producing those golden eggs—producing money—you need to make sure you've created a way to generate the same amount of money coming in. You need to make sure you protect your income and create the ability for that income to replicate itself.

This is why you need to protect your full Human Life Value—not just your current value, but the value of your entire life. People insure their cars for their full value. They insure their houses for their full value. But most people don't insure the thing providing them those assets for its full value: themselves. They often insure themselves only for what they need, versus what their true value is. But ask yourself: if your house burned down, how much house would you want back? If you had a five-bedroom, four-bath house, would you be comfortable only getting a two-bedroom, one-bath house back, because you only really *need* two bedrooms and one bathroom?

If you were in an accident or got sick and couldn't work, you would want to be insured for the same amount of income you would have made if you were working—not just now, but for your whole life. For example, if you are 20 years old, your human life value is 30 times what your current income is. As you get older and approach retirement, your human life value is comprised of your assets at the time—your net worth statement. You want your insurance to cover your full value.

This kind of protection also gives you permission to spend your hard-earned money. If you insure yourself for your full human life value, by the time you reach retirement age, that insurance could effectively double your net worth. If at age 35, when you had $100,000 of income, you insured yourself for $2 million, when you hit $2 million in assets, you are now actually worth $4 million, because you have $2 million in assets and $2 million in protection. Now, you can actually spend that $2 million in assets—because you will still have $2 million in protection to pass on to your family. You can spend all your money, enjoy the fruits of all your labor, and replace all of it to give to the next generation—with no additional out-of-pocket costs.

Don't Change Lanes—Level Up!

As with all the principles in the Freedom Wheel, your *Rules* are designed to grow and evolve as you grow and evolve. As you grow and evolve, your DNA doesn't change—it just levels up. If, when you start out, you are a beginning level investor, as you evolve and as your wealth grows, you level up to intermediate, advanced, super advanced.

Your investment strategy may shift, because strategies can evolve based on better information and better technology. Family trusts can last hundreds of years, so the rules and strategies will inevitably need adjusting and updating. There may be new asset classes, new tax laws, along with new information and technology. But it will still be completely aligned with your InvstDNA™, because your DNA doesn't change.

Often, people will pick a strategy, and then make an emotional decision to change it because of something happening in the market or in their life. But rules really only work if you have them in place and follow them for a long period of time. Changing your rules or strategy is like sitting in traffic and continually trying to switch to the lane that seems to be moving faster. When you chase the traffic line, you almost always end up moving more slowly than if you'd just stuck with the lane you were in. Plus, every time you change lanes, you are exposing yourself to danger.

Instead of changing lanes, level up. When you level up in a game, you don't switch over to playing a different game, you don't switch players, the rules don't change—you just move to a more advanced level of the game. Same rules, same game, same player, higher level—and as you level up, you get boosts and advantages that help you win the race even faster.

Of course, if something truly significant has happened in the lane ahead, like an accident or a lane closure, you may need to change lanes. If you go through a divorce, if you buy a business, if you suffer a death in the family, some things may need to shift. But that doesn't mean the rules of the road suddenly change. It doesn't mean you get out of your car and get into a different car.

For example, we had a client who had done well in life, and then sold his business and all of a sudden had $70 million in liquid assets. We had to adjust some of his *Rules* to manage that influx of cash. We had to tighten some and loosen others. Many people who have a large influx of cash in a short period of time—or even a medium period of time—end up going bankrupt. Lottery winners, NFL players—it happens all the time. Why? Because they never established *Rules* that stood the test of time. They never established *Rules* for the life they want to live. So, when their circumstances changed dramatically, they did not have a rulebook to get them where they wanted to go.

If your *Rules* are based on the life you want to live, they won't completely change even if your circumstances completely change. An influx of cash doesn't change your DNA. Your DNA is who you are inside, whether you make a hundred dollars or a hundred million.

If you stick with your *Rules*, they will evolve as your wealth grows, and they will adjust to your circumstances, no matter what. With your *Rules* in place, you go from the "think" state to the "know" state. You won't just *think* or *feel* you're doing things right, you'll *know* you're doing things right—so you'll *know* you can accelerate forward on your journey to the life you want to live.

Follow this QR code to access bonus content on establishing your *Rules*.

7

EXECUTION

A vision without execution is simply hallucination.

—Scott Jarred

You've figured out your *Why*, assembled your *Who*, laid out your *Gameboard*, and established your *Rules*—but without *Execution*, none of it matters. A vision without execution is simply hallucination.

One of the biggest pitfalls we see in people's personal financial lives is not failing to create a list of things they have to do—most people are pretty good at coming up with a to do list—but actually getting them done. Most of us are busy. We don't have time to adequately research the decisions we need to make. We have other things to do that we are better at doing, such as our jobs and careers. The last thing we want to do with our time is deal with our personal finances.

We can tell you how to reach your full financial potential. We can help you articulate your *Why* and assemble your *Who* and lay out your *Gameboard* and establish your *Rules*. But it's how you act on that information that determines your level of success. It's not the "how to" that's most important, but how you do the "how to." How your strategy is executed (doing) is more important than the strategy itself (how to).

Execution is putting all of your *Rules* and pieces of the *Gameboard* into play to achieve real results. You know where you are headed. You have an amazing team of *Who*s around you, you have all your data organized. But at the end of the day, how are you actually going to execute everything in your path?

Once again, it starts with organization. You have to organize yourself in a way where you can see what needs to be done, where you can see if things are on the right track or not. One of the best ways to do that is with a Financial Life Scorecard™.

The Financial Life Scorecard™

Using the Scorecard, you can check the basic vitals of your financial life. You can check all 20 areas of your financial house, across all four dimensions of your *Gameboard*. You assign a metric to track each one of these, to see if they are working correctly and whether you are moving in the right direction in each of those areas. This allows you to easily identify the most common dangers—such as not saving enough, not having proper liability, having cash sitting on the sidelines not working for you, not refinancing or paying down bad debt, not setting up a family trust—and address them.

Across the four dimensions of your *Gameboard*, there are certain objectives to check on.

For Cash Flow, check whether you are achieving the objectives of:

- Improving cash flow
- Paying yourself first
- Finding lost money
- Reducing cost
- Reducing liability

For Protection, check whether you are:

- Reducing risk
- Protecting your assets
- Protecting your income
- Protecting your life
- Protecting your legacy

For Assets, the checklist includes:

- Higher yields
- Reducing taxes
- Decreasing risk
- Increasing liquidity
- Increasing the rate of return
- Providing income
- Harnessing the velocity of money

And for Liabilities, make sure you are:

- Reducing bad debt
- Utilizing good debt
- Minimizing taxes
- Identifying deferred taxes
- Using debt as an asset

To set the metrics for each of these areas, use the *Rules* you established for each area. Across all of these areas, you can analyze the dangers, opportunities and strengths presented by each one. In each one, there may be an opportunity for improvement. What is the opportunity that could allow you to accelerate even faster? An opportunity could be getting a pay raise, or restructuring your debt, or otherwise finding lost money and putting it back to work. A strength would be having a really good place to put that money, with the best rate of return.

For example, with Cash Flow, we analyze and evaluate how money is coming in and out of your house. In most cases, when we do this, we find 10 to 15 percent of lost opportunity costs which, if corrected, can create $2 to $5 million worth of spendable wealth.

Say we're working with a family that has an income of $100,000 a year. The adults in the family are around 35 years old. On average, we are able to find 5 to 10 percent of lost opportunity costs (money leaking from the household). Recapturing that 10 percent (or $10,000 in this example) and saving it each year would accumulate to $300,000 in 30 years. But if you put that money to work each year at a 7 percent interest rate, that $300,000 grows to just over $1 million.

There were two actions executed that allowed us to create $1 million of new spendable wealth: finding the money that was lost, which created the $300,000, and putting that money to work. Now, that $1 million will generate even more opportunities to create new income streams.

You want to find the money falling out of your net worth—be it through taxes, liability, poor decisions, bad debt, or something else—and redeploy it back into your process to cover the gaps that are preventing you from building the wealth you need. Once that is done, you can create a strategy to build more wealth you can enjoy, to maintain or reduce the amount of risk in your financial life, to protect your wealth under multiple contingencies—and to achieve these objectives with no out of pocket cost.

You want to build additional wealth to give birth to money. You can teach your dollar to do multiple things, harnessing the velocity of money just the way banks do. The goal is for you to become work optional—where instead of you working for money, your money is working for you.

And you want to always be in a defensive position to make sure anything you build is not at risk, and any money you're putting to work has limited exposure to risk. You want to make sure you're protected against tax laws that might change, lawsuits, market crashes, inflation—all those eroding factors. You want to make sure that if you become sick or injured or if you pass away, all your money is protected and goes where you want it to go.

All of this can be done if you *Execute* correctly—if you:

- Get organized and coordinated
- Become a world-class saver by paying yourself first
- Are fully protected so nothing can penetrate the wealth you've built
- Have a war chest of liquidity that can be accessed and deployed at a moment's notice
- Convert debt so it is no longer an eroding factor but can actually be used for arbitrage purposes

If you execute on all these items, you can create $2 to $5 million worth of wealth so you can live the life you want to live, under your own terms and conditions.

Red Light, Green Light

So, how do you make all of this happen? As you go through your Financial Life Scorecard™ with your Personal CFO, you mark each one of these areas—across all the pieces of your *Gameboard*, across all four dimensions—as green or red, depending on whether it is on or off track. Across the board, you identify the issues or dangers that are going to slow you down or stop you in your tracks. If something is marked red, you want to understand why. You investigate what is happening that is causing that area to go off track—and determine what to do to get it back on track.

This is done by working with your Personal CFO to analyze the dangers, strengths, and opportunities of each problem you identify. As you go deeper into the danger presented by the issue, you'll start uncovering opportunities and strengths and can use those to create a new capability.

Say the problem is you're not saving 15 percent, which puts you in danger in the future. Where is the opportunity to improve this area? Perhaps it is in restructuring your debt, which has the strength of giving you more core liquidity.

Or say the problem is you don't have a family trust. The danger is the money could go to probate or to Uncle Sam instead of your family. The opportunity is setting the trust up before your business takes off—which puts you in the strong position of being outside the estate tax transfer system to make your money really work for you.

Once you break down the dangers, opportunities, and strengths of the issue, you can determine the best solution. Then, you outline the next steps—the executable actions—to make that solution happen. These are the *Execution* items on your financial to-do list. Your Personal CFO then passes these *Execution* items on to the *Who*s accountable for those actions. Then, when those *Execution* items are checked off, that area of your scorecard turns green again—that is until you grow and your situation changes and you need to revisit that area to take it to the next level!

As you are accelerating on your journey toward financial freedom, your Scorecard is like the dashboard of a car. You and your Personal CFO check that dashboard to see if any lights pop up indicating something is amiss. Maybe you just need to get gas. Maybe your tire pressure is low. Maybe the check engine light comes on, and then you bring the car in and the mechanic figures out what the execution items are to solve the issue. Your Personal CFO's role is to figure all of that out and fix it—while you are still moving toward your bigger future!

Lifting the Rocks

Along with checking up on these key areas, you also want to make sure you are prioritizing what is most important to you and your family. These priorities are also on your Financial Life Scorecard™—we call them your Rocks.

Say you have a tub you need to fill up with rocks, sand, and water. If you put the water in first, then the sand, then the rock, the rock will displace the water and sit on top of the sand. If you put the sand in first, then the water, then the rock, same thing. You want to put the biggest, heaviest, hardest thing in first—then the next heaviest hardest thing, the sand, and finally the water to fill up the rest of the tub.

Many people get stuck on the water or the sand—all the smaller issues and goals. They get caught up in the nitty gritty, in the nuances, and never end up addressing those bigger issues or goals. When you don't prioritize, you end up feeling overwhelmed by everything there is to do. There are so many little tasks—which one do you start with? Most people start with the easiest stuff, thinking, "I'll get those checked off the list, then I'll move on to the bigger things." The problem is, the little, easy stuff keeps coming. There will always be littler, easier things on the list. If you always do those first, you will never get to the big, important things.

Instead, you should start with the hardest lift first—the big, important things. Those are the things that will really move the needle. What are the three biggest things you want to get done this quarter? What would happen if you just got those three things done?

Businesses often use this strategy, and it forms the foundation of many entrepreneurial operating systems and business programs. If it works so well for business, why wouldn't you use something similar in your personal life? That's why we ask every family who works with us to establish the Rocks they want to take care of—the most important things they want to achieve—and create an *Execution* plan to achieve them.

The Decision Game

You can use this same *Execution* process with every financial decision you want to make. Maybe you want to leave your job and start your own business. The quickest and surest path to financial freedom is business ownership. Many of our clients have followed this path—and those who didn't start out as business owners figured out a way to become business owners in order to accelerate their wealth. You can look at your *Gameboard*, across all the pieces and dimensions, and figure out what you need to do to make that move happen. Then, you can create *Execution* items to make it a reality.

Or maybe you started a business, built it up, and want to sell. The first question is: when do you want to sell? The second question is: What is the value you want to get for your company? Then, you can step back and say, "How do I create that value in my business, so I can exit on my terms, at my price?" Now, you know what you want and when you want it, and you know the levers you need to pull to get there, what *Execution* items need to be handed out and checked off. At Invst, we've helped many clients create value in their business so they can sell when they want, for the price they want, so they can live the life they want.

I could give you countless scenarios where people have evolved and are now growing their capital while simultaneously creating tremendous opportunities for other people. They are mostly work-optional, only working if they want to. They have freedom of time, they have freedom of money, and they are free to spend their time with the people they want, pursuing their passion and purpose.

While you can absolutely stay in your normal career and use these principles and processes to become successful, those who have created another stream of revenue are the ones who accelerate even faster to financial freedom and the life they want to live. Your Personal CFO can help you build and *Execute* that plan.

Whatever decision you are facing, your Personal CFO will take the conversation deeper to really understand what you want and why you want it, and then help you clarify your thinking so you can make a better financial decision.

Then, once you make the decision, who is going to help you get it done? This is where your strategic Board of Directors comes into play.

The Executioners

The biggest problem most people have in executing is they don't have anyone to execute for them. Even if you do have people, you are then responsible for developing the list of problems, solutions, and execution items with all your individual *Who*s, communicating all of that information along with all the relevant data, coordinating who is responsible for what.... And the reality is, you likely don't have the specialization or training to know all those ins and outs. You'll end up spending a huge amount of time dealing with it all.

We met with a client who was looking to buy a second home. To accomplish this, we used their *Gameboard* to weigh and measure the best decisions based on cash flow, assets, liabilities, and protection. We worked with the mortgage broker on the best mortgage combination, we worked with the property and casualty agency, we looked at their investment portfolio to determine the best way to free up money and how to get a line of credit set up. The second home is in a different state with different income tax advantages, so we worked with the CPA to figure that out. For this one decision to buy a house, we collaborated with ten different people to make it happen in the best possible way.

Now, you can do this yourself—talk to all the relevant people on your Board to make sure all the pieces are properly in place. Or you can work with a Personal CFO, who will get all the pieces in place and aligned for you. When you make that decision to buy a house, instead of you having to go talk to your real estate broker and your mortgage broker and your tax accountant and your insurance broker and all the other people in your financial life this affects—you can just talk to your Personal CFO and let them map out your game plan around your *Why* and *Rules* and take care of all the rest.

Instead of having a giant to-do list you have to take care of, your Personal CFO coordinates all those *Execution* items and sends them to the people accountable for executing them. Imagine how simple it can be for you! You don't have to worry about that checklist because your Personal CFO is making sure everything is on track. You can just experience the journey.

Execution is the key ingredient to having a successful financial life—and having someone to help you execute is crucial. With a Personal CFO, you have someone to run point for you, communicating with all of your *Who*s and letting them know what to do. You, as CEO of the household, and your CFO get clear on the problems, solutions, and execution items that serve your vision best. Then, your CFO takes those execution items to the person on your Board of Directors responsible for that action—and holds them accountable to fulfilling those execution items. They are also your personal accountability partner, making sure you are checking off the execution items you are personally responsible for.

And if you don't have the right person on your Board of Directors to fulfill an execution item, your Personal CFO will help you find the right person. At Invst, we have a bench of most trusted advisors who can help you get those execution items done. We've been doing this for over 20 years, and through our work with 2,500 clients we've found the best of the best.

Instead of spending all your time and energy on coordinating all your *Who*s and all the pieces on your *Gameboard*, you can have an expert who is a true fiduciary doing all of that for you, aligned with your *Why*. Then, you can focus on living the life you want. We give you a shortcut to your future. We hack the system so you can reach financial freedom faster.

The *Execution* Accelerant

All of this—the Financial Scorecard™ checkups, problem identification, and analysis, creating *Execution* items around issues and decisions—happens in family meetings with your Personal CFO as part of the Invst4Life™ process. With a Personal CFO, you don't need to have separate meetings with every person on your Board. Instead, you meet with your Personal CFO, who then determines which person on your Board can address the issue.

We do these meetings over and over again, each time looking at each area, making sure everything is on track, and identifying your dangers, strengths, and opportunities for each area. It's like going to the doctor and getting your vitals checked. Is everything working as it should? In each meeting, we go over the execution items and make sure they are all completed and create a new list of execution items based on another round of analysis of all the pieces of your financial *Gameboard.*

After all, you don't only change your oil once the entire time you own a car. You change it regularly, based on how much you are driving. You change out your tires when they get worn down. You bring your car in for regular check-ups, and if something is not working as it should, if something is off-track, if something is slowing you down or putting you in danger, you get it fixed. Maybe your circumstances have changed and you need to change the kind of car you drive. Perhaps you had another child and needed a bigger car. Perhaps you're moving from a warm climate to a cold climate and need to get a car with four-wheel drive that can handle the snow. If you want to keep accelerating on your journey, you have to maintain and update your car—and the same is true of your finances.

That's why we create a cadence of meetings—something we'll talk about more in our next chapter on *Acceleration*—to make sure your financial life scorecard is up to date. And that's why our process is called Invst4Life™—because it is designed to grow and evolve with you over your entire life. It's never static—it is always adapting and optimizing.

This is an ongoing process because as you and your family grow and as your wealth grows, there will be new dangers, opportunities, and strengths, which create new *Execution* items. Having this ongoing process keeps things from getting too tangled and complex, even as your wealth grows. You don't want to hit a ceiling of complexity—you want to bust through that ceiling.

The Ultimate *Execution* Tool

When you *Execute* a decision or solution and move a piece on your *Gameboard*, it affects all the other pieces. Tradition teaches you to employ a micro-specialist (CPA, insurance agent, investment manager, etc.) for each area of your financial life, but this tends to work against reaching your full financial potential. It's like going to three different doctors, each for something different, and having each of them prescribe you a medication. None of them have any regard for how the different medicines will interact. They're only responsible for one issue—no one is considering the side effects on your overall well-being. This can cause you more harm than good.

Your financial life is the same—it doesn't consist of disconnected pieces. Rather, it functions much like the human body. This is the pitfall of the micro-specialist—they can each give you a different how-to, but no consideration is given to the impact on your overall financial health. Doing things this way can limit your financial potential. You must have someone monitoring your overall financial well-being, just like you need one doctor to monitor your overall health.

To successfully *Execute* a comprehensive strategy, you need a framework that can interpret your information—a financial model that teaches you the rules and guides your decision-making process. Now, there's a centralized place where all of that information is automatically updated and disseminated, where your *Rules* can be programmed in, where your *Execution* items can be accounted for, and your *Who*s can have all those pieces at their fingertips. All the elements are connected, and everyone is aligned.

This place is called WealthBuilder™—a platform where your financial *Gameboard* is organized by using innovative technology that produces a real-time picture of your current financial position, your life's work to this point. In your WealthBuilder™ portal, you can see your financial scorecard and *Gameboard* and know exactly where you are, what areas are on track and what are off track, what your *Execution* items are. It's all logged into the system, which uses the power of artificial intelligence combined with the human element to weigh and measure decisions.

This way, your financial model is focused on keeping you optimally positioned for success. It changes as your life does, exposing new threats and stress-testing strategies against your changing information. It can measure the impact of your decisions across your entire financial life before you make them. And it can help you and your Personal CFO outline all the steps to make those decisions happen.

And you know it will all get done because you have your Personal CFO looking at your *Execution* items, looking at your scorecard, holding people accountable for fulfilling those items, and checking them off on your scorecard when they are complete. If someone drops the ball, if something is going wrong, if a piece is missing, you know exactly where to look. You can rest assured that, when all is said and done, no piece is missing. Everything is in place and done correctly in the way that serves you best.

Many people work their whole lives and never get to this place. If you want to put yourself in a position to reach financial freedom and gain your freedom of time, money, relationships, and purpose, *Execution* is one of the most critical principles of the Freedom Wheel™.

Follow this QR code to access bonus content on *Execution*.

8

ACCELERATION

You can't just set and forget your financial life. Without repeatedly recalibrating and making sure you're on track, you will not be able to accelerate into the future.

—Scott Jarred

By the time you reach the *Acceleration* stage, you have peace of mind and harmony, and you are starting to build your value and wealth. Now it is time to focus on the ongoing process of making sure you continue to add value and build your wealth, continue to grow and evolve, continue to live the life you want for you and your family. After all, you don't want to stop being successful. You want to keep growing—because if you are not growing, you're dying.

When you are on a journey, you can't just take one step and expect to get where you are going. You have to keep moving forward, keep refueling, keep taking steps to get to your destination.

Successful people will continue to be successful, but only if they put the work in. If you study the most successful people in the world, their success continues because they have ongoing good habits they stick to. The habits they form help them progress and keep everyone and everything aligned. Unsuccessful people, on the other hand, have bad habits—or no habits they stick to at all.

This is what *Acceleration* is all about: forming good habits to keep your momentum going, to keep your velocity up, to keep you thinking abundantly instead of getting stuck in scarcity. And this is a habit-forming process we know will work—because we've seen it work over and over again. It's not like a fad diet, where most people fall off the wagon almost as soon as they start. Weight loss and health require more than just a diet—you need other healthy habits like exercise and a good sleep schedule. You need the whole, comprehensive health package. That's what will keep you fit longer—and the same is true with your finances. This process is designed to keep your finances healthy, to protect and sustain the health of your wealth, so you can continue to build and grow.

Part of staying healthy is re-calibrating based on where you've been, where you are, and where you need to go next. Without understanding where you are, there is no way to make sure you are still on track to get where you want to go. If you don't take the time to reset, think back and have gratitude for what has happened, and re-calibrate for the future, you can quickly slip into scarcity mode without even realizing it. *Acceleration* is about staying in that abundance mindset.

Without understanding where you are, there is no way to make sure you are still on track to get where you want to go.

So, how do you keep moving in the right direction? How do you make sure you are keeping the momentum within your financial life moving in the right direction, not letting your finances—or yourself—get stuck in place? Through quarterly meetings called Perfect 10 Reviews™.

This is where you get your car in tune so you can continue to accelerate toward your goals. You're getting your oil changed, you're making sure everything is aligned so you can hit the gas and move forward confidently in the right direction. This is what keeps the wheels turning, what keeps your journey moving forward, and it's what will catapult you to the next level over time.

The Perfect 10 Review™

Acceleration is all about meeting cadence—forming the habit of having regular, recurring, productive meetings that assess your whole financial life both thoroughly and efficiently. This is what the Invst4Life™ Perfect 10 Review™ does. We call it the Perfect 10 because, just like in gymnastics, we are aiming for a perfect score in these meetings. We want to:

- Have a step-by-step agenda, with actionable items
- Make sure the vitals of your financial strategy are in place and on track
- Check in on your *Why*—has it changed?
- Look into the future and see what you really want to happen
- Ensure your *Gameboard* is still organized
- Reaffirm that your *Who*s are aligned
- Make sure your *Execution* strategy is working
- Check that your *Rules* are being followed by everyone

These are your state of the union meetings, your chance to recalibrate. They give you a framework to assess whether everything is working or not, what your dangers, opportunities, and strengths are in the present moment and in the future. If there are obstacles in your way, this is the time to create execution items to address those obstacles. What are the most important things you need to accomplish to help you move forward? What do you, your CFO, and your Board of Directors need to work on between now and the next meeting?

We want to get all of this done—and we want to do it in 60 minutes. You are busy. You have a lot going on. This shouldn't be something that takes up a huge amount of your time! So, instead of having many meetings every quarter with all the different *Who*s on your Board, trying to get all the pieces into alignment, bouncing back and forth between different people with different agendas, you have one quarterly meeting with your Personal CFO where you address everything at once. With this one quarterly meeting with your Personal CFO, you can keep your entire financial life on track and accelerate toward your future.

We want to be both efficient and thorough, so we have a tried-and-true agenda you can use as a framework to make sure you can cover everything within 60 minutes. That agenda looks something like this:

Family Headlines – 5 minutes

You start with your Family Headlines—the big things happening within your immediate family. This is where gratitude comes in, as you look back at the major things you've accomplished.

- Where are you currently with your family?
- What's working?
- What did you do really well?
- What are some big wins you've had in the last quarter that you can be proud of?

You look back into the future, assessing how well you did and where you're moving. You should always be grateful for what you had before while simultaneously moving forward. After all, without looking back and seeing what you and your family have done, how can you see what your future will hold?

You have to take the time to focus on your wins as you move forward. Gratitude actually helps you accelerate.

From there, you look to the future—starting with your destination, your *Why*.

Why For Money and Top Three Lifetime Achievements – 5 minutes

In order to get where you want to go, you need to make sure the destination on your GPS is still correct. When you are younger or early in your journey, what you want to achieve in your life can be very foggy. As you get older and closer to that goal, you start to see it more clearly and often have a different perspective. As you are evolving and accelerating, building velocity and abundance, you get more clarity on what you really want. And as you get closer to that destination, it usually becomes clearer and easier to articulate—and it may take on a new form.

Often, as people start becoming successful and growing more quickly, the picture of the life they want to live becomes even more grand and beautiful. They realize that initially, they were thinking too small, and they can dream bigger.

That's why you always revisit your *Why* for money and your top three lifetime achievements you want to accomplish.

Three Years from Now: What Has to Happen – 15 minutes

Once you've looked at your destination, you zoom in on your near future. You look three years into the future and see what the world looks like for you, where you want to be—and what could stop you from getting there.

- What are the dangers you might face in the next three years?
- What are the opportunities you can seize?
- What strengths do you have right now that can help you get to where you want to be in three years?

Breaking the future down into three years gives you the ability to recalibrate. Every quarter, you can check and see whether you are still on track, whether your vision of where you want to be in three years has changed, whether it is still what you really want.

Most important 12-month financial priorities – 5 minutes

Every year you set a one-year target, and every quarter you assess and reset based on your progress toward that goal, and any changes that might shift that goal.

This is the part of the meeting where you talk about the Rocks we discussed in the last chapter—your most important financial priorities for the next 12 months, the things you really need to knock out. How are they being addressed? Maybe one of your Rocks is buying an investment property or a rental house or second home. You and your Personal

CFO put together the *Execution* items you need to get that one big goal done: making sure you have enough cash on hand, making sure your income is in the right place, working with a broker to find the right piece of property, talking to the mortgage broker to find the right mortgage, etc. Then, each quarter you assess how you are progressing toward accomplishing this goal.

Your Rocks are the three to five really critical things that if you get them knocked out in the next 12 months, you'll be in great shape!

Gameboard: Are You on Track or off Track? – 10 minutes

Next, you look at your *Gameboard* to:

- Evaluate whether your protections are in place and on track
- See whether you're in a good position when it comes to taxes, or whether there is more you could do
- Look at cash flow to make sure:
    - You are saving the right amount to hit those work optional numbers
    - Your cash flow index is under control
    - Your debt-to-income ratio is balanced
    - You have no bad debt, only good debt

You also go through your investment position and look at your InvstDNA™ to:

- See whether your investment portfolio is performing as well as it can based on your investment policy statement, or whether anything is falling outside your guidelines

- Check whether your investment policy statement is being followed
- Make sure you are still on balance

Your investments can quickly get out of balance if something is not done well, or if you are making decisions that are not aligned with your investment policy statement.

You also make sure you are on track for becoming Work Optional, using our Work Optional Playbook™—a formula based on your age to know whether you are on track to become work optional.

YOUR TOTAL INCOME	
EARNED INCOME	
PEOPLE AT WORK TOTAL:	
MONEY AT WORK	
Interest:	
Dividends:	
Royalties:	
Passive Income:	
Real Estate Net:	
Business Net:	
TOTAL MONEY AT WORK:	

ARE YOU WORK OPTIONAL?				
MONEY AT WORK		WORK OPTIONAL NUMBER		GAP
$50,000	-	$100,000	=	-$50,000
	-		=	

For example:

- At 30 years old, if you have five times your earnings saved, you would be 25 percent of the way to work optional.
- At 40, with 10 times your current earnings, you would be 50 percent of the way there.
- At 50, if you want to be 75 percent of the way to work optional, you would need 15 times your earnings.
- At 60 years old, you would want 20 times your earnings to be able to have 100 percent of your income replaced.

Dangers, Opportunities, Strengths list – 5 minutes

Then, you list out your dangers, opportunities, and strengths:

- What are the opportunities you have coming up?
- What are your strengths that will help you get there?
- What strengths do you need to work on?
- What are the dangers that are standing in your way?

Execution Items – 10 minutes

Next, you go through *Execution* items—all the little steps you need to knock off those Rocks and to get anything that is off track back on track. Some of these *Execution* items may be things for you to do, or for your Personal CFO to do. The rest your Personal CFO distributes, along with any necessary information, to the person on your Board responsible for that piece.

Rank meeting – 5 minutes

Finally, at the end of the meeting, you assess whether the meeting was productive or not. The only way you can understand how valuable and productive a meeting was is to have a ranking system. In a perfect world, all of your meetings would be as productive as possible—a perfect 10 out of 10. That's what we shoot for—we don't want your financial review to be unproductive for you! These quarterly meetings should be some of the most important meetings of your year.

If the meeting was not a Perfect 10, we have a scoring process to find out exactly where it fell short, what can make it better, what *Execution* items need to happen to get us to that Perfect 10. You set certain goals, metrics, rocks, execution items at the last meeting—did you accomplish them? If the execution items from the last meeting were not completed, that lowers your score. If the Rocks have still not been knocked out, that lowers your score. If you just spent the whole meeting rehashing what you talked about last meeting, that meeting would not get a very good score. After all, the definition of insanity is doing the same thing over and over again with the same result. Each meeting, you want to see growth and forward movement. You want to see *Acceleration*.

As Steve Spurrier famously said, "You are whatever your record is." Ranking your Perfect 10 Review™ is a way of keeping record, keeping score of how your financial life is doing. If you don't have a scoring mechanism, how do you know how well you are doing? Ranking gives your Personal CFO a way to be held accountable to the results they should be getting for you. By ranking the meeting, you can say, "That was not a productive meeting, and

> **"You are whatever your record is."**
> **- Steve Spurrier**

here is exactly why. Here is what we need to do to make the next meeting a Perfect 10. Here are the things we need to think about. Here are the execution items."

At the end of the day, it's not Invst's financial life—it's yours. Invst is in the value creation business, and we want to make sure this process is valuable, productive, and working for you.

The P10 Scorecard™

As you go through this agenda, you enter each piece of it into a form, and at the end of the meeting, you have a one-page document that sums up the entirety of the meeting: your family headlines, your Rocks, your dangers, opportunities, and strengths, your *Execution* items, your meeting ranking.

Also included in this document is the scorecard we talked about in the last chapter. As you go through this agenda, you take that scorecard, assess whether each area is green or red, and if it's red, analyze it, make *Execution* items, and delegate those items to the person on your Board responsible.

This is also where you make sure your *Who* are holding up their end of the bargain, making sure their piece is working in the right way. The scorecard allows you to see when something is not happening and where you need to follow up. In between meetings, you and your *Who*s should accomplish the *Execution* items established at the meeting and distributed by your Personal CFO. At the next meeting, you see if all those execution items are completed or on track. Are your *Who*s getting the results you want? Do they really understand what you want, and do they really want to help you? Are they dropping the ball? If they are, it may be time to reevaluate their position on your Board.

Every quarter, you are evaluating your most trusted advisors to make sure they are still the right people for your Board. As you are accelerating, you are growing, and sometimes the people you started with may not be able to take you to the next level, due to their capacity or skillset or skill level. It's not necessarily a bad thing—for whatever reason, they may just not be equipped to handle the next phase of your growth. If that's the case, you can create the execution steps necessary to let that person go and find the right person to fill that spot on your Board.

Meeting Cadence

You should be doing some kind of checkup like this at least annually or every six months, but we have found the most successful process is to have these meetings quarterly. Each quarter, there will be a different set of things to address based on the needs of that quarter. For example, in the first quarter of the year, you'll spend more time looking at your *Why* and whether you need to revisit or revise any elements in that slice of the Freedom Wheel™. The next quarter, you may spend time on your virtual *Gameboard* and making sure you are positioned properly. In the meeting at the end of the fourth quarter, you'll address what needs to be done for tax time, which is coming up in the next quarter. This cuts things into bite-size components, quarter by quarter, as you move toward your lifetime goals, your vision, and the life you want to live.

Every major corporation has a quarterly report, in which they assess the present position of the company, whether everything is on track, where they want to go, and recalibrate how they are going to move forward. This is standard practice for successful businesses, and history has shown it works.

If it works that well for a business, why can't you do the same thing for yourself?

The Perfect 10 Review™ provides a framework to make sure everything that needs to get done is getting done when it needs to get done. It is the perfect process to evaluate, weigh, measure, and understand whether everything in your financial life is being handled properly. Without these quarterly check-ins and recalibrations, your financial life can quickly get out of alignment. Your values can get tilted.

We often see this in families under financial stress, where spouses aren't talking about finances. They're not level setting. They're out of alignment. This can happen as you start speeding up, which is why it's so important to continue these meetings even as you are accelerating. Things are working at a more rapid pace than you are used to. These meetings are a chance to reset your levels, to get yourself back in alignment.

Part of *Acceleration* in the Invst4Life™ process is creating repeated tasks you can work on and get better and better as you go—creating those good habits that ensure success. If you do Perfect 10 Reviews™ for 50 years, and you have 200 quarters of Perfect 10 meetings, that's just 200 hours of your time for a lifetime's worth of wealth and productivity. That's a pretty good trade!

The Road to *Why*

As you *Accelerate*, your *Why* has to stay on pace with your new speed. The most successful people in the world always envision what the future holds. They see what they want in the future, they clearly articulate it, they recalibrate as they journey toward that future, and they get everyone rallied around them to reach it.

My friend Bryan Neale is a great example of how this kind of process plays out. Bryan always loved football, but he didn't quite have the athletic prowess to make it to a high level of playing the game professionally. He knew he would never make it to the NFL as a player, but his dream was still to have a career in the NFL—so he set out to become an NFL referee. But he didn't just set that goal for himself—he mapped out where he wanted to be on his career path by certain points in his life.

Bryan started on this path when he was 19. By the time he was in his early 40s, he wanted to be in the NFL. And by age 51, his goal was to be a referee in the Superbowl. He had a vision of where he wanted to go, he set metrics for himself, he regularly assessed whether he was hitting those metrics, and adjusted his plan accordingly. And in 2022, at age 52, he was a referee in the Superbowl.

Bryan knew his career path as a referee would not make him much money, so he had another career as the owner of a coaching program to support himself financially. By managing his finances correctly, he was able to put himself into a position to take advantage of the refereeing opportunities that would take him all the way to the Super Bowl.

Bryan accomplished this using the same type of visioning process we use, envisioning where he wanted to go and what it would look like to get there. There aren't many people who have been Superbowl refs—it's not an easy goal to achieve! But Bryan was able to hit that target because he was very clear on his vision. He was able to articulate it and create an executable roadmap to get there.

This is what Invst4Life™ creates for your financial life: an executable roadmap that you revisit and recalibrate as you progress on your journey. If you are able to articulate where you want to go, what you want your life to be, you can make your money work for you to help you get there. You can be where you need to be financially to make that dream a reality.

Your finances aren't your *Why*—they are the fuel that helps you get to your *Why*. Not having your finances in place can hold you back from your true *Why*. The goal is not to make you wealthy for wealth's sake, but so you can reach your lifetime dreams and goals and live the life you want to live.

Recalibrating Your *Why*

Of course, 52 is far from the end of someone's life. Bryan had reached his life goal of being a ref in the Superbowl, but now he has so much more life ahead of him. Now, he can envision what his next goal will be and set a new destination in the GPS of his life's journey. Invst4Life™ allows you to recalibrate as you evolve—and gives you the financial security to stay on track even as you take new opportunities and forge new paths.

If your heart isn't in something anymore, you'll never be able to stay on track. Your destination has to be your true passion, your true *Why*. I know a doctor who was a pediatric surgeon. It's what he went to school for and what he practiced. As he practiced, his passion for helping children grew, and he decided he wanted to pivot and go into pediatric orthopedic care. To do that, he had to go back to school, leaving his family for two years to return to his studies. He recalibrated his *Why* and reinvented himself—at the age of 50.

Just because he was a doctor doesn't mean he was automatically in a financial position to leave his job and return to school. He was making a good income as a pediatric surgeon, but he knew in order to follow his *Why* he needed to take that time off to reinvent himself. So, he worked to put himself into a financial position where that was possible. Now, this doctor is changing children's lives even more than he was before—including my daughter's.

This reinvention can happen at any time and can be as big a recalibration as you need it to be. It's never too late to find your passion and follow your *Why*. I know an obstetrician in Tampa who started out as an engineer, but after witnessing the amazing work of obstetricians during the birth of his children, realized he wanted to help women in the same way. So, he left what he knew, went back to school, and became an obstetrician, completely reinventing himself. He's now in his 60s and is truly living his *Why*, even opening an institute devoted to obstetric practice. But in order to do this, he needed his finances to be in a place where he could afford to leave his career as an engineer and go back to school.

It's never too late to find your passion and follow your *Why*.

A traditional financial plan doesn't have this kind of reinvention and recalibration factored in. It doesn't have space to adjust and grow and evolve your *Why* as you grow and evolve. Invst4Life™, on the other hand, is designed to grow and evolve with you.

We've found that once our clients amass wealth, their *Why* includes using their money to help others and contribute to the greater good, so they start giving it away to charities and foundations and to support those in need. If they use the financial *Gameboard* and set everything up the right way—such as becoming the beneficiary of their own life insurance—they can literally give away all their money if they want to and then replace it entirely to give it back to their family. They can make a huge impact in whatever way they want while continuing to grow and accelerate throughout life. Whatever path they want to follow, they will have the option to do so.

My wife's uncle is the owner of Wild Birds Unlimited, now the largest seller of birdseed in the world. He started selling birdseed out of the back of his van and created bird feeders and smart ways to move the bird seed, and now he has grown to the point where he can give his money back to the cause he is so passionate about: conservation. He buys golf courses that would otherwise be developed into residential buildings and gives them back to the city to convert into nature preserves. He followed his *Why* all the way from the back of his car to making a huge difference by creating huge conservation spaces for wildlife. Without having a *Why* aligned with a smart financial model, it would be impossible to deliver that kind of impact.

Accelerating the Wheel

Acceleration is what keeps the whole Freedom Wheel™ turning. Each of your Perfect 10 Reviews™ builds on the last, and the Freedom Wheel™ becomes a flywheel that keeps spinning faster and faster, building and growing and generating more opportunity. That's how we build *Acceleration.* If you set and forget your financial life, it won't work. Without repeatedly recalibrating and making sure you're on track, you will not be able to accelerate into the future.

As our clients build and grow, as they come to us with good ideas and opportunities, we want them to invest in their dreams and reach success. We want you to continue to grow and evolve and build—to always be *Accelerating* forward. That's why we call our process Invst4*Life*™: because it is an ongoing, lifelong journey—and it's what brings all six principles of the Freedom Wheel™ together.

Follow this QR code to access bonus content on *Acceleration.*

9

Putting the Wheel in Motion: The Invst4Life™ Process

You are the CEO of the financial institution we are building together.

—Scott Jarred

The Invst4Life™ process focuses on you, your family, and your future, and it is how we put the six principles of the Freedom Wheel™ into action. With Invst4Life™, we use those six principles to:

- help you discover your unique abilities and your *Why* for money
- define your lifestyle objectives
- execute a financial gameboard
- create a model to weigh and measure financial decisions

- analyze your present position
- discover your dangers, opportunities, and strengths
- assemble team of trusted advisors around you
- evaluate your exposure to risk
- identify gaps in protection
- discover your human life value and how to protect it
- compare what-if scenarios
- analyze your current cash flow
- find your lost money and redeploy it to create velocity
- establish rules for your money and people to help you execute them
- learn your InvstDNA™ to apply rules to your investment strategy
- create a personalized investment policy statement
- develop a framework to guide financial decisions with innovative technology that produces real-time pictures of your life's work
- accelerate through monthly webinars, quarterly seminars, and Perfect 10 Reviews™

Throughout this whole process, you'll have your Personal CFO to help you along the way.

Reaching your full financial potential is a process, and Invst4Life™ is designed to educate, guide and counsel you toward that end. So, let's take a look at how that process works.

Onboarding Invst4Life™

At the beginning of Invst4Life™, you'll have the opportunity to go through a discovery process for yourself. This starts with a Total Financial Life Checkup™: a confidential financial questionnaire before your first meeting, which covers the six principles of the Freedom Wheel™ and scores how you rank in each of those categories. Perhaps your *Who* is super strong, but your finances are unorganized and missing pieces, so you score low on *Gameboard*. Perhaps your investments are great, but your protection is lacking. We use this as a starting place so you can discover what key principles need work. Then we start to gather the most important details to build your *Gameboard* and assess your current financial position.

One thing we will never evaluate you on is the size of your checkbook. We evaluate you based on whether you love yourself, your family, want to grow, want to think abundantly, and want help to do so. It doesn't matter to us how much wealth you have when you start. We are simply taking the financial decisions you've made up to this time, aligning and organizing those decisions, and coordinating that information so we have a clear picture—an MRI if you will—of your financial life. Once we understand you, we can make adjustments that will help you reach financial freedom faster. Understanding your current financial position and your mindset today will help you get to a better tomorrow.

Once you have completed the questionnaire, we move into a series of onboarding meetings.

Meeting 1: You, Your Family, Your Future

The first meeting is all about you: finding your *Why*, understanding it, digging deep and discovering your vision for yourself and your family, and articulating clearly what you want your bigger future to be.

Those first meetings are a unique time for most people. We rarely get time to sit and think thoroughly and clearly about what we really want. Even more rarely do we get the opportunity to figure out how to articulate what we want in a clear, concise way. Even if you've read a multitude of the self-help books out there about discovering your passion and purpose, most people have never actually sat down and done the work to think it through.

This is exactly what happens in the first meeting. You design what you want your future to be. You're busy. You're running around doing everything you need to do, usually focusing on everyone but yourself. Now is your chance to spend some time on *you*.

And for the first time, you have a Personal CFO who is facilitating your thought process, helping you write the story of what you want, asking the questions that will take you one level deeper so you can find even more clarity. They ask questions that get you into the right frame of mind to imagine what is possible. Most people don't ever get the opportunity to do that, which makes this first meeting one of the most impactful meetings of the whole process. It's an exciting and uplifting chance to design what you want your future to be.

In this meeting, we have four objectives:

- Get to know you
- Give you the opportunity to get to know us
- Discover your *Why* for money, articulate your values, and start to see your vision for your dream life
- Identify our role in your journey—how we will be side by side with you, helping you write the story of your life

Getting to your *Why* is what we'll figure out as we go through this journey together. If you can get clear on what you want, you can get clear on the challenges and obstacles that are standing in your way and how to overcome them. You can get clear on the opportunities and strengths that will get you to where you want to be. These are all the things you will dig into in the next four meetings of your Invst4Life™ onboarding—the financial underpinnings of how to make that happen, how to reach that goal, how to build the car that will get you to your *Why*.

Meeting 2: Gameboard

In the next meeting, you'll set up your virtual financial *Gameboard*, creating a model to analyze your present position, measure your decisions, discover your dangers, opportunities, and strengths. You'll empty out that financial junk drawer and get all the pieces organized, making sure everything is in the right position and checking to see if there are any pieces missing.

Once your *Gameboard* is set, we show you how to understand it and use it, going over which pieces have what powers and how they work. You'll look at all four dimensions of the Gameboard: assets, liability, cash flow, and protection.

You'll also lay out your *Who*, your Board of Directors, and make sure you have the right people in the right place. You'll identify who is going to help you with each of the components of your *Gameboard* and build out an accountability chart. You'll also compile a list of questions to ask your team of advisors, to make sure they are aligned with your *Why* and can truly help you get where you want to go.

With your *Who* and *Gameboard* set up, in the next meetings you can establish the *Rules* your *Who* and *Gameboard* will abide by. Every piece on your *Gameboard* will have a set of rules that we will develop together, which will tell us how to operate as an organization—with you as the CEO and us as your CFO.

Meeting 3: Protection

The third meeting focuses on protection. This is where you go into all the "What If" scenarios:

- What happens if you get in a car accident?
- What happens if you get sued?
- What happens if your house burns down?
- What happens if you and your business partner don't get along and split up?
- What happens if you become disabled or ill and can't work?
- What happens if, heaven forbid, you die prematurely?
- How does your protection hold up across all the different things that could happen to you?

Of course, we don't want this meeting to be all doom and gloom. We just want to make sure you are protected from the unforeseen. How do you make sure your financial future is secure regardless of things that are out of your control?

We do this in part by determining your Human Life Value and making sure you are properly insured for that value while eliminating unnecessary coverage and making sure you are buying protection the best way. You should be able to protect yourself fully without adding any additional out of pocket costs!

Protection is one of the most overlooked areas of opportunity in your financial life. Most financial advisors don't pay attention to this dimension. They are focused on getting your money and holding on to it for as long as possible, so they create products and strategies to do that. And the advisors who do spend time on protection usually have no clue how to really use it to help you reach financial freedom faster.

As the saying goes, defense wins championships. Protecting yourself against the unforeseen is what allows you to take advantage of opportunities when they arise. Protection is also the thing that can create the most opportunity, through methods like becoming the beneficiary of your life insurance, which is a way of using protection to allow you to enjoy your wealth longer and more fully. (You can read more about how this works in *#FutureHack!*.)

Protecting yourself against the unforeseen is what allows you to take advantage of opportunities when they arise.

Meeting 4: Cash Flow

Once you have your protection in place, we focus on cash flow. Cash flow is the fuel for your journey. It is the lifeblood of your financial life. If you get a blood clot, you're dead—or at the least, your health is severely negatively impacted by a heart attack or stroke. The same is true for your money—the fuel for your journey to the life you want to live. You need to keep your money flowing in the right way. You want to create a system for the movement of money, to channel that power so it is always working for you.

We start by analyzing your current cash flow. Once you understand your current cash flow, you can find lost money and put it back to work, utilizing the velocity of money to make your dollars do multiple things at once.

The velocity of money allows you to use money in multiple different ways so you can always take advantage of those opportunities because your dollar is always doing multiple things at once. There are many ways to use velocity of money to get multiple streams of income to build wealth, the same way banks do, while still leaving a legacy for your family.

(Once again, if you want to learn more about this, check out *#FutureHack!*, where I delve into velocity of money in more detail!)

As we discussed in Chapter 6, most people's cash flow is out of order. If your cash flow is out of order, your money is going to erode. You'll have less money to work for you in the future, so you will always be working to provide for yourself and your family. You'll never be able to live the life you want because you'll always be running on that wheel.

You want to make sure you are taking care of yourself first. You want to make sure your cash flow is optimized to protect you and scale in the right order as you grow. So, you and your Personal CFO set *Rules* around how much you save, how much you spend on protection, how much you put toward paying down your debts, and how much you have left over for lifestyle. As you go across the dimensions of your cash flow, you set rules and parameters that will help you optimize, scale, and grow as you build your wealth.

To do this, we have a software platform that optimizes your cash flow called your Wealth Building Account™. When money comes in, it is deposited into that account. We then program the account to automatically redistribute your money according to the *Rules* we set together. This way, you can make sure you are automatically paying yourself first.

It's almost like every dollar has a binary code, and it is programmed to do something when it comes to you. If you don't have your money programmed to work for you, it will go to work for someone else. With the Wealth Building Account™, every dollar is programmed to go where it needs to go: savings, protection, long-term investments, expenses, lifestyle, emergency fund, tax account, child's college account. You can rest assured that your money is finally working for you, doing what you have planned for it, not what somebody else has planned for it.

When your cash flow is optimized, money comes into your world. As your money builds, you get dividends, interest, opportunities in real estate and business, and you can adjust how your cash flow is redeployed.

Meeting 5: Investment

One of the places we program your dollars to go is into your investments—the focus of the final Invst4Life™ onboarding meeting. In this meeting, you'll look at where your money is invested today—which may not be in the right place or aligned with your values.

This is the meeting where you learn your InvstDNA™. You'll go through a process to help you identify your InvstIQ™ to understand your investments, your InvstEQ™ to understand your emotions around investing, and InvstXQ™ to understand your experience with investing. With your InvstIQ, EQ, and XQ we create your InvstDNA™ profile—just like taking a personality test to discover your personality type. Then, based on your InvstDNA™, we establish an investment strategy that works for you. We create the rules for your investing—what in the industry is called an investment policy statement—which dictates what happens with your money that goes into investments. We then program each dollar going into your investments to automatically go to work for you, based off your InvstDNA™.

The vast majority of financial firms out there won't do investment policy statements for the average individual investor. We want to change that. We believe it's just as important for a family to have an investment policy statement as it is for a financial institution. We don't see why there should be any difference.

Ultimately, we believe one person or group of people should not be treated differently than another person or group of people. I'm not saying we're the only financial firm that believes this—but most don't have the means, the technology, the processes in place to make it happen. We've created a process that allows you to discover your InvstDNA™ for yourself—and have a written report of it, your investment policy statement, to base your investment strategy on.

Invst WealthBuilder™

Over the course of these onboarding meetings, you will set up your Invst WealthBuilder™ portal, an app that organizes your entire financial life in real time. It aggregates all your financial data so you can have your financial *Gameboard* at your fingertips. You can see your protection, your net worth, your current and future cash flow, all in one spot. It's very easy to understand and intuitive to use.

Many of the financial information aggregating systems or asset management systems out there today pull information for the purpose of selling you a product. That's how financial institutions work—they have their own agenda. WealthBuilder™ is not trying to sell you any product. It works to optimize you and put you in a position to make smarter decisions. You should be able to go to one place and find out all your most important financial information. You should know your credit, your network of advisors, how everything is working together, and how we make sure they're coordinated and making aligned decisions to get you where you want to go.

WealthBuilder™ updates automatically on a daily basis, aggregating all your financial information from all relevant sources into one place. You can see a daily scorecard—no different than checking the scoreboard during a game. You can access all of your most up-to-date documents and net worth statements at once, as well as outlined projections of your cash flow, future taxes, investments, debts. You can see how they all interact, create a current snapshot of where your financial life is now, and project out the path you are on.

All of the information on the WealthBuilder™ portal is completely confidential, protected with top-level encryption. Your Board of Directors also has access to your WealthBuilder™ portal (within appropriate privacy constraints), so they have access to all the information they need as they work on your behalf.

Acceleration

These five onboarding meetings take place over the course of your first 90 days of the Invst4Life™ process. After those 90 days, your financial life is organized and optimized. You have a whole financial ecosystem built. You discovered your *Why*, you organized your information on your *Gameboard*, you worked through your protection, cash flow, and investments. You've found lost money and put it back to work. You've built a wall and a moat around the castle of the life you are going to build. You established your *Rules* for money, so your *Who* can *Execute* with confidence.

90 days after you complete these meetings, you'll have your first Invst4Life™ Perfect 10 Review™ to assess where you are. From there on out, you'll go into the regular *Acceleration* meeting cadence of quarterly Invst4Life™ Perfect 10 Reviews™ to keep you accelerating into the life you want to live.

In the Invst4Life™ process, *Acceleration* expands beyond meeting cadences. We manage your virtual gameboard on a daily basis, keeping track of what is happening through our tech stack here at Invst, making sure those dollars are working while you sleep, that your money is always in motion, accelerating you toward financial freedom and the life you want to live.

Plus, you get access to a suite of interconnected apps and platforms. For example, you can connect with other Invst4Life™-ers, plug into a wealth community based on principles and values, and ask questions anytime with our InvstIQ™ financial wellness platform.

You can also connect through our monthly Invst4Life™ webinar series, WealthShops™, which give you the insights, resources, and tools to expand your financial knowledge and reach your goals quicker. WealthShops™ topics include everyday areas of your financial life like taxes, investing, protection, estate planning, setting goals, vision boards, family legacy, mortgages, eliminating debt, velocity of money and so much more.

There's so much financial misinformation out there—on television, online, even in the newspaper—and we usually have no real idea of how it applies to us. Instead of just sending you information that may or may not be applicable to you, these webinars are purposefully designed around the six key principles of the Freedom Wheel™ built for you, your family, and your future. We take that information and align it with a principle to demonstrate how it is (or isn't) applicable to you. They are designed so you can actually take what you learn and put it into practice.

When you start the Invst4Life™ process, you become part of the tribe, part of the community, and you get access to all of these resources and information. Instead of just listening to the news or what people are saying online and trying to parse what it means for you, these webinars and this community are a place to go where everyone speaks a common language and shares common principles and values.

And all of this is just some of the ongoing education and support we offer as part of the Invst4Life™ process!

Get To Know Invst

As you can probably tell, at its heart, Invst is in part a FinTech company. Many technology companies eventually become irrelevant and outdated because newer technology is invented that makes older technology obsolete. The technology we use is simply to support proven principles and a proven process, to make them more effective and efficient. When new, better technology is developed, we use that technology. The principles and process stay the same, because they stand the test of time.

But Invst isn't just about using the best technology to get the best results. We believe financial services always require actual human beings as well. We can use technology to be faster and more efficient, but you still have to have the human touch for it to really work. Invst is like a cyborg—we have the highest-quality technology stack, along with human beings with emotional intelligence and empathy who help deliver you the best results to get you to financial freedom faster. That's why our Invst4Life™ process is not just about us getting to know you—it's also about you getting to know us.

So, who is Invst? We make money work for people so that they can live the life they want. Our goal is not to represent the financial institutions, it's simply to make money work for people. If a strategy or product doesn't do that, we are out.

The strategies we offer are based on proven principles that will stand the course of time. The people who work at Invst are hired and fired based on core values and accountability, not on large bureaucracies and org charts. This allows you and us to grow at a faster rate because we have clearly identified the true value of money—which is far more important than money itself. Values give us the vision to take you all the way to the finish line—and beyond.

Our Values

We have core values that are central to our business—central to helping people reach their full financial potential. Our philosophy is built on these core values, which align with yours.

Always Growing: We believe in your highest potential. When you work with us, we'll show you how quickly your growth can rocket. At the same time, our team is always growing and learning for your benefit.

It's critical to work with a team that understands the importance of separating fact from opinion. Our strategies are based on principles, facts, evidence, and time-tested philosophies with proven results. Knowledge is power. We never stop learning—we never stop improving. Our technology delivers your financial information to you in a faster, more efficient way than you may have ever experienced. Harnessing your information in real-time, in one location, allows you to capitalize on that collective knowledge. Because of this, you can continuously optimize your current financial position, and make smarter financial decisions.

Batteries Included: We wake up everyday feeling energized with passion and purpose for serving you in living the life you want. We also ask you to bring your batteries to make your vision a reality.

This is your financial life. No one else's. This means you have to be in the driver's seat, you must play the leading role. You are the CEO of the financial institution we are building together—your job is to make the critical decisions in your own interest, to understand what is being done on your behalf, and to bring all of yourself to the table.

This is your financial life. No one else's.

WITWOWWOW (Whatever it takes, without whining, while only winning): Whatever it takes to help our clients live the life they want, without whining but instead with an attitude of gratitude and service, while only winning, because we don't believe in losing.

We are your CFO—our job is to help you weigh and measure your decisions—to educate, guide, and counsel you toward reaching your full financial potential. Sitting on the same side of the table as you means we both need to agree on the strategies we're going to implement. If we don't agree, as your fiduciary I work directly for you, not for any financial institution, so you can clearly state what your needs are. Your input is as important as mine. We're not here to write our story—we're here to guide you to write *your* story. We act in the best interest of our clients and always maintain the highest level of honor, sincerity, and forthrightness.

Abundance Mindset: We see the world as plentiful and we're here to help you take advantage of it. That also means that you don't have to wait for retirement to fully enjoy your life.

Reaching your full financial potential isn't about how much money you have or don't have. It's about whether or not you're willing to cultivate the right mindset that will help you live the life you want. Success isn't prescribed to only a select few, as we all have the same potential. The difference is that successful people understand success takes what it takes—they understand that the way they think about their everyday actions, and choices they make, will either push them forward or weigh them down. Reaching your full financial potential starts with your mindset. Therefore, we give you the tools and resources to cultivate a mindset for success.

Always Got Your Back: When you hire us, you hire our entire team, regardless of who is your Personal CFO. We're all here for you on your best days and your worst days, too.

We're not in this business for ourselves. We're a team whose core passion is to help people, to make one of the most significant differences in your life. Money is stressful—whether you have a lot or a little. Finances are complex. But you deserve to reach your full financial potential, to live the life you want.

That's why we will always have your back, making money work for you. Times will get tough. Markets will change. Unexpected life events will occur. When you are thrown those curveballs, we are there to help you get through them—or even take advantage of them. And we will be there when the world throws you incredible opportunities to help you make the most of them.

Personal Integrity: We do what we say we're going to do. Because we know so much personal information about our clients, we must always operate with the utmost integrity.

The only place our loyalty lies is with you, our client. Our standing as a Registered Investment Advisory firm places us as a fiduciary to you. It means we're not tied to large institutions, or broker-dealers who command our loyalty to them over you. Our team represents you, your best interests, and works for you alone, no one else.

As an independent firm, we have created an environment outside of Wall Street conformity. You won't find any stuffy board rooms or fancy suits when you meet us. Instead, you'll find a team of people who roll up their sleeves and go to work for you every day. You'll find a team whose passions are to make money work for people and to empower people to make smarter financial decisions.

A Proven Process

To us, wealth management isn't just about managing your money—it's about managing information and then programming your money to go to work for you and building wealth. As Warren Buffet famously said, "If your money doesn't work while you sleep, you will be working for the rest of your life." You only need to commit a few hours of your life to hack the next 10, 20, 30 years of your future.

Invst4Life™ is a proven process and a proven system that will help you accelerate to the next level. We know that if you follow these principles, this process will work over time. We see it across the board with our clientele. Over the course of working with close to 3,000 households, completing these quarterly meetings every year, we see their trajectory skyrocketing. They are growing far more quickly than they were before they started working with us. They're becoming work optional more quickly. They're making the right decisions as they move forward.

The Invst4Life™ process works because it is always moving, always living and breathing, always working for you, as long as you live. It works because it is built around you, your family, and your future. It works because it helps you articulate what *you* want, and helps you get there. It works because it eliminates the stress and fear around money—allowing you to accelerate your journey all the way to financial freedom and the life you want to live.

Follow this QR code to access bonus content on The Invst4Life™ Process.

Ready to Accelerate?

If you've reached this point in the book, I'm sure you have come to see the value of having a principle-based system that will help you accelerate your life. I bet you are ready to get that dream destination programmed into your GPS, fuel up and make sure everything is ready for the journey, get an all-star team assembled, and set out toward your bigger future.

If you are, I'm happy to tell you that you've already taken the first step, simply by reading this book. You are already in the mindset of making a change to your financial life. Now, it's time to take action. It's time to say, "I'm in."

The best way to start accelerating is to start the Invst4Life™ process. You won't find a process like this, driven by principles and evidence-based strategies, with a Personal CFO who will be by your side the whole time, anywhere else. It simply does not exist anywhere else—and you're lucky enough to have found the only place you can get all of these elements in one place, making sure your money is working for you, following principles and a process that will stand the course of time for you and for generations after you.

Part of accelerating is the ability to realize what you want and take immediate action to make it happen. If you want a tree, the best time to plant it was twenty years ago. The second-best time is right now. The sooner you take action, the better. The sooner you get your money working for you, the faster you can become financially free.

Studies show that if you are inspired to take action and don't do so within 48 hours, you never will. You can't sit on this. If you do, it will pass you by. Make the decision to accelerate—right now—by heading to Invst.com to take the Total Financial Life Checkup™. You can take this quiz no strings attached. Then, if you are ready to begin your journey to financial freedom, you can start the Invst4Life™ process and meet with a Personal CFO who will take you through this journey. In 90 days, you'll be on your way to financial freedom and the life you want to live.

Now is your chance to jump on board with a process, a team, a community, and a movement that will help you get there faster. Now is your chance to stop stalling, feeling like you're never getting ahead, feeling like others are always speeding past you. Now is your chance to stop living in scarcity, second guessing your decisions, wondering if you are going to be okay. Now is your chance to find freedom from fear and financial worry. Now is your chance to reach financial freedom faster so you can live the life you want.

Now is your chance—to *ACCELERATE.*

Endnotes

1 "60% of Americans Now Living Paycheck to Paycheck, Down from 64% a Month Ago," LendingClub, February 28, 2023, https://ir.lendingclub.com/news/news-details/2023/60-of-Americans-Now-Living-Paycheck-to-Paycheck-Down-from-64-a-Month-Ago/default.aspx.

2 Sarah Foster, "Survey: More Than Half Of Americans Couldn't Cover Three Months of Expenses With Emergency Savings," Bankrate, July 21, 2021, https://www.bankrate.com/banking/savings/emergency-savings-survey-july-2021/.

3 Jack Flynn, "20+ Shocking American Savings Statistics [2023]: Average Personal Savings Accounts, Demographics, And Facts – Zippia," *Zippia* (blog), February 16, 2023, https://www.zippia.com/advice/american-savings-statistics/.

4 Alessandra Malito, "Nearly One-Third of Older Americans Have Less Than $10,000 Saved for Retirement," Barron's, June 22, 2022, https://www.marketwatch.com/story/nearly-one-third-of-older-americans-have-less-than-10-000-for-retirement-11655834396.

5 Kristen Beckman, "58 Million Americans Have No Retirement Savings: How Employers Can Help," BenefitsPRO, February 16, 2023, https://www.benefitspro.

com/2023/02/16/58m-americans-have-no-retirement-savings-how-employers-can-help/.

6 "New Report: 40% of Older Americans Rely Solely on Social Security for Retirement Income," National Institute on Retirement Security, January 14, 2020, https://www.nirsonline.org/2020/01/new-report-40-of-older-americans-rely-solely-on-social-security-for-retirement-income/.

7 Dan Sullivan, "The 4 Freedoms That Motivate Successful Entrepreneurs," Strategic Coach, https://resources.strategiccoach.com/the-multiplier-mindset-blog/the-4-freedoms-that-motivate-successful-entrepreneurs.

8 Dan Sullivan. *Deep D.O.S. Innovation: Create Unique Value for Your Clients by Helping Them Transform Their Dangers, Opportunities, and Strengths.* Author Academy Elite, 2020. www.strategiccoach.com

9 EOS Worldwide. "The People Analyzer." https://www.eosworldwide.com/people.

10 Dalio, Ray. *Principles: Life and Work.* New York: Simon & Schuster, 2017.

11 Sullivan, Dan, and Dr Benjamin Hardy. *Who Not How: The Formula to Achieve Bigger Goals Through Accelerating Teamwork.* Carlsbad, California: Hay House Business, 2020.

About the Author

Scott Jarred grew up in Indianapolis in Section 8 housing and on food stamps. Despite being poor and afraid, the hardships he experienced did not crush him. Instead, they motivated him to figure out how to make opportunities happen.

After spending years working in corporate America, Scott left to build a company committed to making money work for people and to flip the traditional wealth industry on its head. In June 2016, he became the CEO of Invst, a company he founded with Lloyd Easters to provide comprehensive wealth management solutions for high-net-worth individuals to protect and preserve their wealth.

Invst has created an environment outside of Wall Street conformity, one that's broken through the limitations of "financial planning" and instead focuses on financial positioning. Scott is dedicated to providing faster, smarter, and innovative personal wealth solutions for his clients.

Scott enjoys living his best life with his wife and three children.

Connect with Scott at ScottJarred.com.

The Accelerate Advantage

Discover proven principles to Accelerate your wealth.

(So you can live the life you want!)

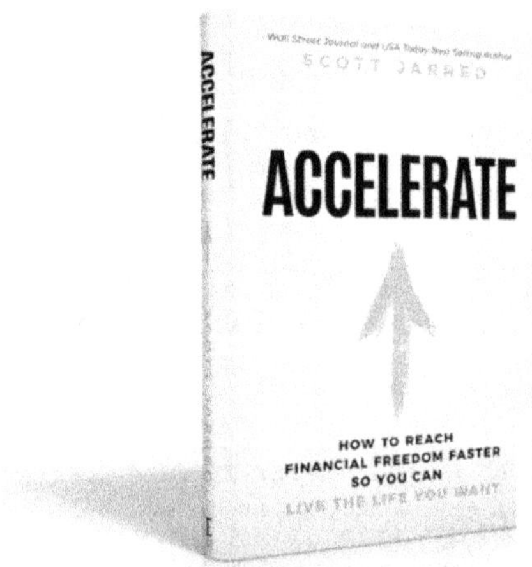

Scan to register and receive several bonuses available only to Accelerate readers.

About INVST

MAKING MONEY WORK FOR PEOPLE

When I left corporate America to start my career more than a decade ago, I made myself one promise: I would build a company committed to making money work for people. I quickly learned the industry has its own agenda. I discovered that advisors are more focused on pushing products, rather than taking the time to evaluate the long-term impact on the person's life. I quickly learned that in order to truly make a difference, we had to be an industry transformer, to flip the traditional hierarchy on its head. Thus, INVST was born.

Growing up and even as a young adult, I was living in a scarcity mindset. I've experienced the constant grind and struggle of chasing the dollar, never feeling like I had enough. So before I could make a difference in people's lives, I had to change the way the traditional industry taught me to think about money—the way they teach all of us to think.

I had to break through the ceiling of my mind's limitations and view my life through the lens of abundance. I went to self-improvement and business coaching seminars, read every book I could get my hands on, and learned how the wealthy think about and make money.

Having an abundance mindset is asking how you can accomplish anything you want by putting your resources to work for you. Successful people aren't defined by their environment—they make their environment a product of their influence. This is at the heart of what we do for our clients. First, we make money work for people, ensuring that your resources are working toward accomplishing your state objectives. The My CFO Series helps you create a financial environment that furthers your most important goals and aligns your actions with your values. It's an environment that gives you the necessary tools and resources to make smarter financial decisions so you can live the life you want.

To learn more, visit Invst.com.

invst™

MAKING MONEY WORK FOR PEOPLE

Reach financial freedom faster

Follow us

THIS BOOK IS PROTECTED INTELLECTUAL PROPERTY

EASY IP™

The author of this book values Intellectual Property. The book you just read is protected by Easy IP™, a proprietary process, which integrates blockchain technology giving Intellectual Property "Global Protection." By creating a "Time-Stamped" smart contract that can never be tampered with or changed, we establish "First Use" that tracks back to the author.

Easy IP™ functions much like a Pre-Patent™ since it provides an immutable "First Use" of the Intellectual Property. This is achieved through our proprietary process of leveraging blockchain technology and smart contracts. As a result, proving "First Use" is simple through a global and verifiable smart contract. By protecting intellectual property with blockchain technology and smart contracts, we establish a "First to File" event.

Powered By Easy IP™

LEARN MORE AT EASYIP.TODAY

Printed in the USA
CPSIA information can be obtained
at www.ICGtesting.com
JSHW010244270824
68820JS00007B/8/J

9 781636 802060